FIGHTING HISLAM

WOMEN,
FAITH AND
SEXISM

FIGHTING HISLAM

SUSAN CARLAND

MELBOURNE
UNIVERSITY
PRESS

MELBOURNE UNIVERSITY PRESS
An imprint of Melbourne University Publishing Limited
Level 1, 715 Swanston Street, Carlton, Victoria 3053, Australia
mup-info@unimelb.edu.au
www.mup.com.au

First published 2017
Text © Susan Carland, 2017
Design and typography © Melbourne University Publishing Limited, 2017

This book is copyright. Apart from any use permitted under the *Copyright Act 1968* and subsequent amendments, no part may be reproduced, stored in a retrieval system or transmitted by any means or process whatsoever without the prior written permission of the publishers.

Every attempt has been made to locate the copyright holders for material quoted in this book. Any person or organisation that may have been overlooked or misattributed may contact the publisher.

Cover design by Sandy Cull
Typeset by Megan Ellis
Printed in Australian by McPherson's Printing Group

National Library of Australia Cataloguing-in-Publication entry

    Carland, Susan, author.
    Fighting Hislam/Susan Carland.

    9780522870350 (paperback)
    9780522870367 (ebook)

    Includes index.

    Sexism—Religious aspects—Islam.
      Muslim women—Conduct of life.
      Muslim women—Social conditions.
      Women in Islam.
      Sexism in religion.

297.082

CONTENTS

Dangerous Waters   1
One   Beyond the Harem   11
Two   Witnesses to their Faith   37
Three Journey to the Fight   61
Four   Encouragement, Hostility, Apathy   85
Five   The Double Bind   107
Six   The Third Way: Faith and Feminism   123
Changing the Narrative   141

Acknowledgements   147
Glossary   149
Notes and Sources   153
Bibliography   161
Index   175

DANGEROUS WATERS

Within minutes of arriving to collect my professionally bound thesis, I found myself on the receiving end of an unsolicited and impenetrable rant about female genital mutilation.

'What's your paper on?' the shop owner had inquired.

'It's on Muslim women an—,' I began, but before I could finish my sentence, he had launched into the subject. That I hadn't even mentioned the words 'female genital mutilation' was irrelevant; merely saying 'Muslim women' was wide enough a rabbit hole for him to dart down. My presence as a Muslim woman and my half-delivered topic were the only encouragement required for him to pontificate.

That he felt authorised to deliver a lecture to me about his understanding of the allegedly sexist treatment of women in Islam, the very subject on which I was there to collect my years-long PhD dissertation, didn't even surprise me anymore. This was not the first time a stranger had felt entitled to raise the potential religious-interference of my genitals with me. Many years earlier, amid the cadavers and preserved body parts trapped in perspex boxes during an anatomy tutorial at university, my teacher had merrily joked in front of the class about me undergoing genital mutilation, given I was a Muslim.

I was less shocked at this more recent encounter, but both times I was mortified and angry. It's uncanny how often people will try to demonstrate their concern over the alleged oppression of Muslim women by humiliating them. Even finding out the details of my research findings didn't seem to do much to deter people from baldly sharing their opinions on Muslim women.

When I was neck deep in my doctoral research, I attended a black-tie, journalism-industry dinner on a windy Sydney night. In the well-dressed crowd were some of Australia's most intelligent and perceptive thinkers. By this time, I had grown accustomed to answering questions about my subject. I had also grown quite used to the standard responses I received to my thesis, and so I habitually gave ambiguous answers to avoid these reactions.

A well-known and popular journalist approached me and asked what I did for living. His reaction, despite belonging to a group of people usually known for their cognitive skills, was so representative of the myriad reactions non-Muslims gave to my research subject matter that I scribbled it down on a dinner napkin as soon as he left, so I would not forget a word:

>Journalist: So what do you do?
>
>Me: I'm completing my PhD.
>
>Journalist: On?
>
>Me: *(Purposefully vague)* Sociology and politics.

Journalist: But what is your exact research question?

Me: *(Inward sigh at what was inevitably to follow, but valiantly indifferent exterior)* I'm investigating the way Muslim women fight sexism within Muslim communities.

Journalist: *(With widened, alarmed eyes)* That's dangerous waters!

Me: *(Through gritted teeth)* Not really. It's been going on for many hundreds of years, and I've been spoiled for choice with the number of women who have been willing to be participants in my research.

Journalist: Did they want it known, what they were doing? Or did they need it kept secret?

Me: *(Icy frustration descends like Arctic winter)* Oh, many of them were happy to be identified in my research. In fact, some were angry when I suggested giving them a pseudonym, insisting they wanted to be known for this work.

Journalist: *(Now completely flabbergasted)* But … but, did their husbands know of their apostasy?!

Me: *(Choosing to ignore use of 'apostasy' as eyes take on glacial sheen)* Actually, many of the women listed their husbands, or another Muslim man like their father or imam, as their greatest supporters.

Journalist: *(Now quite literally speechless)* … !

I've had similar exchanges—too many to count—with non-Muslims over the course of my research. Commonplace is the firm conviction that sexism against Muslim women is rife, most often coupled with the utter disbelief that women who challenge sexism could exist, let alone that there are many of them, that they are not a new phenomenon, and that Muslim men often support them in their efforts. People rarely make any effort to hide their feelings on the topic—indeed, they see no reason to. As far as they are concerned, their beliefs are based on 'fact', and the situation for Muslim women is dire. I often wonder how they can be so comfortable presenting these attitudes directly to me, a clearly identifiable Muslim woman in a hijab (headscarf). They do not appear at all uneasy in making it apparent just how bad they think life is for any and all Muslim women, and how unengaged they believe Muslim women to be in confronting the sexism they invariably face.

I have received similar, but different, reactions within some sections of various Muslim communities when they found out the focus of my research. Often I would be purposefully vague when discussing my topic with them, too. I would restrict myself to saying that I was researching 'Muslim women', and avoid highlighting the 'fighting sexism' part, as there is a complicated, often suspicious attitude towards anything that may be perceived as 'feminism' within Muslim communities. Or I would rush to reassure them that I was not framing this in an anti-religious perspective.

Their scepticism is perhaps an understandable reaction from a minority community that frequently feels under siege, particularly when it comes to women's rights. I hoped the fact that my research was being carried out from within a common faith, and that it drew explicitly and deeply on the theological resources afforded by this, reassured them that I, unlike many others, was not engaging in an attack on the faith and communities they held dear. But still certain people within the Muslim community are scornful, rolling their eyes and calling me a feminist—not as a compliment, but a warning. They saw feminism and Islam as inherently at odds.

This is the terrain in which my research into Muslim women occurred. The subject is fraught on multiple fronts, and the expectations and beliefs of people from all sides provide a glimpse into the environment my participants inhabit. It seems that the topic of 'Muslim women and sexism' is a minefield of unflappable certainty and indignation from all corners. Yet for something about which so many people are adamantly sure, I feel there is very little information from the women actually involved. It seems to me that, in the argument in which Muslim women are the battlefield, the war rages on and the angry accusations zing past their heads from all sides. The main casualty is, ironically, women's self-determination.

Islam is arguably the most discussed religion in the West today, in both media and society, and, after terrorism, the plight of Muslim women is probably the most controversial topic of debate. I have been asked, challenged, harangued and abused about 'Islam's treatment of women' countless times in person and online. Nonetheless, there is only a small amount of published work available on the topic of Muslim women fighting sexism within Muslim communities, and much of that focusses on women who see Islam as inherently part of the problem—if not the whole problem—that Muslim women face. That is, Islam is the cause of the sexism they experience, and thus Muslim women need to be extricated from the religion entirely before anything close to liberation or equality can be achieved.

There are limited sociological accounts of Muslim women who fight sexism from a faith-positive perspective, and only a handful of studies that investigate the theological works of, some Muslim feminists. The responses to, and motivations of, the women are dealt with coincidentally, as opposed to primarily. This small pool of available resources clashes with what I know anecdotally to be happening in many Muslim communities, as well as the historical accounts of Muslim women who have been challenging the sexism they have experienced from the earliest days of Islam by using religious arguments.

I was vexed—and rather surprised—at the inexplicable paucity of information on a topic that is so debated. In order to address this significant gap, I conducted research among Muslim communities in Australia and North America in 2011 and 2012. As part of this research, I interviewed twenty-three Muslim women. They were theologians, activists, writers and bloggers, and all of them were engaged in fighting sexism within their various Muslim communities. I looked into the motivations of and responses to the women in my study, and then considered the religious and ideological inspirations, tensions and struggles they had in their line of work. My research was feminist in its methodological approach, in that it privileged women's lived realities, and committed to amplifying and recording the lives and experiences of Muslim women. Thus the historical and theoretical accounts I wanted to provide were woven around the words and experiences of my participants.

While at times I felt my writing was pedestrian to the point of the painfully obvious, early non-Muslim readers assured me that the candid and deeply personal accounts of the women I interviewed were indeed new and surprising to them, reinforcing not just how important it is that their stories be shared, but just how scant such information is to many. That, coupled with the dizzyingly regular encounters I have with people possessing an entitled combination of arrogance and ignorance on the topic of Muslim women, convinced me that the topic is indeed one worth pursuing.

For years now I have been speaking on issues relating to Islam, Muslims and gender to the media, both Australian and overseas. In one sense I choose this, but in another it has been chosen for me, moulded by the way others attempt to define and restrict me, more or less obliging me to respond. It's a common story. Jasmin Zine, a Canadian scholar, once observed that not just our actions but also our very identities are constantly being shaped by dual, competing discourses that surround us. There's the fundamentalist, patriarchal narrative, persistently trying to confine the social and public lives of Muslim women in line with the kind of narrow, gendered parameters that are by now so familiar. But there are also some Western feminist discourses that seek to define our identities in ways that are quite neo-colonial: backward, oppressed, with no hope of liberation other than to emulate whatever Western notions of womanhood are on offer. This wedging chimes with my experience, and it's a problem because, as Zine argues, both arms deny Muslim women the ability—indeed the right—to define our identities for ourselves, and especially to do so within the vast possibilities of Islam. It is as though male Muslim scholars and non-Muslim Western feminists have handed down predetermined scripts for us to live by. And it is left to those people thought not to exist—female Muslim women who fight sexism—to rewrite those scenarios and reclaim our identities.

Like the women I've interviewed, my very existence is one of 'talking back' to assumptions and generalisations so often made of Muslims. There's nothing homogenous about Muslims or the conditions in which they live. Such assumptions, as associate professor of religious studies Sa'diyya Shaikh says, are an 'intellectual, political, and popular idiom' that need to be rejected precisely because they are so pervasive in portrayals of Islam.

It is important for you to know where I'm coming from. 'Researchers cannot have "empty heads",' is the way Gayle Letherby puts it. We're obliged to 'acknowledge intellectual and personal presence' in our research, especially when we have so much in common with those we're researching. Clearly, I am approaching the topic as an insider. I am a Muslim woman researching the experiences of Muslim women. No doubt there's some bias to that, but it's an illusion to think outsiders don't have biases of their own. What is often assumed to be the outsider's 'objectivity' is really a sceptical subjectivity. In truth, both perspectives have things to offer. Insiders can easily decipher what they see and hear, which is especially valuable in something as laden with codes and symbols as religion. Insiders are also likely to be given greater access, and the women I interview will be prepared to be more candid with me—to disclose things they simply wouldn't to another interviewer. And while it's true that some things may best be observed from an outsider's distance, I feel we are almost drowning in those observations right now. If anything, we live in a society where the only views that seem to matter and which are given prominence in relation to Muslim women are the most distant. This book exists because the voice of insiders has long been ignored.

There are also ways in which I am something of an outsider to the women I interviewed. I am a different nationality to all the North American women I interviewed, am younger than many of them, and I am white, unlike the majority of the interviewees, and therefore an outsider to the experience of being a woman of colour. The truth is far more nuanced than simply being either an insider or an outsider. It is not a dichotomy at all, as it is not static. An individual can shift between the two positions in a single piece of research, and even be both at the same time, depending on the issue at hand and the person being interviewed.

This is a project born, ultimately, from frustration. Since becoming Muslim as a teenager (and to pre-empt you: no, not to get married. How telling the default conjecture is that the only possible explanation for a Western woman to become Muslim is to appease a man; that it could be through personal, independent conviction is seemingly inconceivable), I have watched the conversation on the topic of Muslim women and sexism develop only incrementally. The obsession with the hijab persists, and Muslim women are still spoken of largely through the prism of unchallenged oppression. Similarly, Muslim communities still struggle to face sexism head on. Many mosques have inadequate space for women, domestic violence still occurs, women are excluded from leadership positions, and some people feel a Muslim woman speaking about women's rights, even from a solidly religious basis, is suspect at best.

I recall being given an award for my work within the Muslim community many years ago, and as part of my prize I was invited to address a large room of Muslim leaders. I used the opportunity to speak out against the way Muslim women were treated at many mosques, with deficient space, inadequate access and hostile treatment from the men who ran the mosques. I framed my entire argument in classical Islamic sources, and pleaded not for a deviation from, but a return to orthodox Islamic practice of welcome inclusion of women in the mosques. Even then, a number of men stormed out of the room, mid-speech, in protest. And yet, even with these failings occurring on all sides, I knew—from my own experience, and that of the many wonderful Muslim women around me—that sexism was being challenged all the time within the Muslim community.

That this situation isn't widely acknowledged exasperates me to the point of wanting to tear out my hijab-covered hair. When I think, or am asked, about this topic now I feel a weariness start to envelop me in a way that I have not previously. It is very disheartening to look back and realise that, nearly twenty years since becoming Muslim, we are still on the same carousel of unsophisticated and demeaning assumptions from all sides about my faith and a woman's place in it. I don't want my daughter or my son to be answering the same questions or face the same battles as me in twenty years time. So doing this research and compiling it is, at the very least, something they can point people to when asked about the topic of Muslim women and sexism.

I want to provide an accurate snapshot of the lives and experiences of Muslim women who are engaged in fighting sexism within their traditions and communities, and are doing so with the resources that their faith affords them. They do not need me to 'give them a voice'—they have their own, and always have. But in a world that seems adamant to talk over them or about them—to pretend they are not there, do not matter, are too confused to contribute meaningfully, or have no voice—I hope this book provides a much-needed account of their work, in their own words.

One
BEYOND THE HAREM

> Even my secular understanding of what feminism is, there's not a competition with what Islam says, and women's role in it. To me, there's a correlation, and not a conflict.
>
> — *Umaymah*

Muslim women have a mixed history of engaging with sexism. It is built upon resistance, victimisation, endurance and complicity, and must be understood as emerging from a long series of interactions: of Muslim women being (both the real and imagined) victims of sexism, as well as the respondents to sexism. This history has led to the current situation and informs the landscape in which all Muslim women, including the women I spoke to, operate. Like women everywhere who encounter sexism, sometimes we quietly accept it because we see responding as futile or even aggravating, sometimes we angrily fight back, demanding our rights and our dignity, and sometimes we quietly work in the background, delicately negotiating the obstacle course of ego and cultural tradition. I have done all these things, both within and outside of the Muslim community, and will probably do so until the day I die.

The grim reality of living in a patriarchal world means your gender is always a ghost that hovers over every situation. Women learn early on, as little girls, that being female is never irrelevant—it always has its consequences. In order to understand this in the context of the Muslim community, it is useful to have at least a brief overview of the history of Western views of Muslim women,[1] the history of Muslim women fighting sexism with the resources and perspectives available to them within Islam, and a history of the issues with the term 'feminism' in some Muslim communities.

Classical Islamic law affords women the same right and obligation to an education as it does to a male, the right to financial independence (in both earning and spending, including owning property, entering contractual agreements and initiating enterprise), the right to keep her name after marriage, the right to sexual satisfaction from her spouse, the option to use contraception if she desires, the right to divorce, the right to initiate and refuse marriage, the right to be a religious authority equivalent to men, the right to social and political participation, and the right to financial maintenance from her husband, as well as viewing her as a spiritual equal to men. It even states that a woman is not required to serve her husband food or clean his house.

Despite the rights and status that Islam confers upon women, many in the West have associated Islam with the oppression of women since at least the eighteenth century. Much of this belief was fuelled by the Western fascination with 'the harem', which 'though often prurient, placed a high premium on renditions of the segregated world to which Western men were not permitted entry' (Lewis and Micklewright, 2006). This fascination created a lucrative market for 'inside the harem' accounts, written by both Western and Middle Eastern women.

Significantly, even in the early 1900s, Muslim women who had lived in the Ottoman Empire were railing against the non-Muslim accounts emerging about harem life for Western audiences. So, for instance, Zeyneb Hanoum (a pen name for Hadidje Zennour), an upper-class Ottoman Turkish Muslim woman, announced 'that nine out of every ten books on the harem should be burned' as they were so erroneous. In turn, she wrote her account of the reality of living within a harem to redress that imbalance. Compare this with the modern avalanche of hand-wringing declamations of the plight of Muslim women, and it soon becomes evident that the phenomenon of publishing misinformation and outright fantasies about Muslim women for eager Western consumption is nothing new.

The negative view of the treatment of Muslim women has persisted over the centuries, though its form has changed somewhat. Muslim women were generally seen as the inverse of the Western ideal of womanhood. Thus, in Victorian times, when Western Christendom championed a puritanical, chaste view of women, the Muslim woman was viewed as the lascivious, sex-hungry temptress. Her veil was seen as a form of enticement, and the harem was viewed as a hotbed of unbridled sexuality. The staged pornographic photos taken of 'harem girls' during this time fuelled this perception and were incredibly popular, despite the fact that they were often fakes.

Now that the West prides itself on the freedom of women and its open view towards sexuality, the Muslim woman is seen as oppressed and deprived of autonomy, as little more than the 'passive embodiment of exotic suffering' (Morey and Yaqin, 2010)—her veil now restricts her movement and denies her sexuality. In the Western imagination, the Muslim woman perpetually embodies 'the other'.

The belief that Islam is inherently oppressive towards women has often been coupled with the expressed desire to rescue the

Muslim woman, even if against her will. This is well illustrated by Lord Cromer, the British Consul-General to Egypt (1883–1907), who announced back in the late 19th century, 'I am here to liberate Muslim women, I am here to liberate them from Islam'. The desire to free Muslim women from Islam, whether they like it or not, is coupled with the belief that the only explanation for Muslim women's adherence to Islam is, as anthropologist Saba Mahmood describes it, a form of 'false consciousness or the internalization of patriarchal norms through socialization'. That is, no clear-thinking woman would ever choose Islam as a way of life; it is something imposed upon her by a confused state of mind or lack of exposure to viable alternatives. Thus, the inevitability of the liberation of Muslim women from Islam is seen as natural, as Muslim women are little more than 'pawns in a grand patriarchal plan', and if they are 'freed from their bondage' they would 'naturally express their instinctual abhorrence for the traditional Islamic mores' that enslave them.

The dubious desire to free the Muslim woman from herself still exists. The most recent incarnation is the Feminist Hawk, as started by writer and psychologist Phyllis Chesler, which openly 'advocates the use of force to liberate Muslim women from persecution and burkas [sic]'. Its driving principle is the struggle against 'islamofascist misogyny'. The idea that Muslim women need rescuing from their woefully sexist predicament is therefore alive and well, if only because there is a complete lack of belief that any woman would be Muslim if given another option. After all, why would they support something that seems to be harmful to them, 'especially at a historical moment when these women appear to have more emancipatory possibilities' (Mahmood, 2005)?

The desire to free Muslim women didn't spring from misplaced paternalism. The 'plight' of Muslim women has, though, been used to rationalise invasions into Muslim-majority countries, such as Afghanistan, when, for instance, the then First Lady Laura Bush made the unusual move of taking over her husband's weekly radio address to highlight 'the plight of women' in Afghanistan as it 'is a matter of deliberate human cruelty carried out by those who seek to intimidate and control'. This speech was echoed two days later by Cherie Blair, wife of then British Prime Minister Tony Blair, who also spoke publicly and at length about the lack of women's rights in Afghanistan. These speeches were widely viewed as part of a campaign to bolster support for the invasion of Afghanistan, linking Muslim women's emancipation to the need to bomb the country.

These negative attitudes towards Muslim women can be understood in the broader context of Islamophobia. This term has existed at least since the 1980s, though some reports date it as early as the 1920s. The pioneering academic engagement with the concept came from the race equality think tank The Runnymede Trust in 1997, who stated that the term is 'not ideal, but is recognizably similar to "xenophobia" and "Europhobia", and is a useful shorthand way of referring to dread or hatred of Islam—and, therefore, to fear or dislike of all or most Muslims'. So, negative attitudes towards Muslims—and specifically towards Muslim women—are not new phenomena in the Western world, even if the term Islamophobia is arguably less than 40 years old. However, several commentators have noted the increase in anti-Muslim, anti-Islamic sentiment in the West, to the extent that 'in the global "West", the racialized "Muslim Other" has become the pre-eminent "folk devil" of our time' (Morgan and Poynting, 2012).

There is little doubt that the alleged treatment of Muslim women in Islam concerns non-Muslims living in the West considerably. A 2005 Gallup Poll of US households found that 'gender inequality' was among the top responses American women gave to the open-ended question, 'What do you admire least about the Muslim or Islamic world?'. The Muslim women I interviewed were acutely aware of the way non-Muslims view them, throughout history and in modern society. Indeed, it would be hard for them not to know, when Muslim women's attire and Muslim women's rights (or lack thereof), constantly make the headlines.

Muslim women are aware, particularly if we wear the hijab, that we are never anonymous, and our existences are never benign. Every action is interpreted as pregnant with patriarchal meaning. When walking along the street with my husband, I know to never dawdle in his wake while window shopping or daydreaming, as falling a step behind is perceived by onlookers not as accidental but an active embodiment of my inferiority to him. When my husband spoke adoringly about me in an acceptance speech for an award he was given, non-Muslim friends later contacted me saying how great it was to hear a Muslim man speaking respectfully about his wife. It was seen as remarkable only because it was not assumed to be the default. This awareness cannot help but shape the way my participants engage with sexism within their own communities—particularly, their determination to fight the very sexism many outsiders thought was part of their religion, with religion.

Far from passively waiting around for some external force to liberate them, much less being somehow complicit in their own oppression, Muslim women have actively fought for their rights, both by participating in theological debate and by challenging the sexist status quo since the advent of Islam. Sometimes this struggle was carried out within an explicitly religious framework, other times it was not. However, all are endeavours by Muslim women to fight sexism. While it would be impossibly ambitious to give a full account of more than 1400 years of attempts to challenge patriarchy across many homes, villages, cities and countries, I do want to offer a sense—for that is all that it can be, given the richness of the tradition—of some of the more notable efforts on the part of Muslim women.

Ibn Kathir (d. 774) narrates the story of the woman of the Quraysh tribe who used the Qur'an to argue publicly with 'Umar (the *caliph* or ruler of the time) only a few years after the death of the Prophet Muhammad. 'Umar wanted to cap the value of the *mahr*, a gift that must be given to a woman for her personal use. The woman criticised his plan using Qur'anic verses to justify her disagreement, and upon hearing her argument, 'Umar rescinded, saying 'The woman is right and 'Umar is wrong'. Other reports exist about female companions of the Prophet Muhammad approaching the Prophet to initiate divorce from their husbands, to request education when men were blocking their opportunities, and to complain about domestic violence.

Women contemporaries of the Prophet Muhammad and his immediate successors were also engaged in Qur'anic interpretation, especially on verses pertaining to justice or rights of women. Aisha and Umm Salamah (both wives of the Prophet Muhammad) were recorded as doing so, and around 150 years after the death of the Prophet Muhammad, the mother of al-Shafi'i[2]—himself one of the greatest religious scholars in the history of Islam—is recorded to have challenged a judge over his treatment of her while she was in court, basing her argument on a Qur'anic verse specifically referring to women. Aisha is also known for issuing *fatawa* on numerous issues, but is especially renowned for giving rulings that reminded people not to view women negatively when there was no religious basis to do so. In one instance, when a rumour was circulating among some Iraqis that a woman and lowly animals passing in front of a praying man would spoil his prayer, she declared, 'Listen, oh people of Iraq. You think that a donkey, a dog, a woman and a cat passing in front of a man praying cuts [ruins] his prayer. You have equated us women with them?! Push away whoever comes in front of you as much as is possible for you. For nothing cuts the prayer.' Another version of this ruling has Aisha criticising the man who was circulating this lie, saying to him, 'You have made women like the worst animals!'

Sakina, the Prophet Muhammad's great-granddaughter and a personal favourite of mine, put conditions in her marital contract that would scandalise a modern Muslim community, such as the right to commit *nushuz* against her husband, and that her husband, Zayd, would never go against her will. When Zayd was once foolish enough to do so, she took him to court and in front of the judicial bench shouted at him, 'Look as much as you can at me today, because you will never see me again!'

Many accounts of Muslim women from the medieval period point to their large numbers in scholarship, trade and positions of influence, including slave women. In a groundbreaking English-language account of traditional female Islamic scholarship, author and compiler Mohammad Akram Nadwi states there were numerous instances of women teaching *hadith* classes to students, both male and female, in principal mosques and colleges from the sixth century AH[3] on; 'issuing *fatwas*; interpreting the Qur'an; challenging the rulings of *qadis*; criticising the rulers; preaching to people to reform their ways'. These actions were approved and applauded. 'The sheer number of examples from different periods and regions … establish that the answer to some of the "If men can, why can't women?" questions is "Men can and women can too"'.

All the women I have interviewed were actively involved in challenging sexism when and how it was presented to them. Unfortunately, many Muslim women's endeavours have been lost because they simply were not recorded in written form, but were limited to the oral tradition. A major shift occurred around the nineteenth century, when Muslim women moved from being the objects of cultural writing to its subjects. It was from the nineteenth century, when women started to write their own journals, form organisations with the explicit rubric of feminism, and record their own histories, that a tangible and cohesive Islamic feminism emerged at a national level in places like Egypt. It was at this time that both individual and collective activism began to take place, whereas previously it had nearly always occurred individually. Although there are many instances of this activity in places like Morocco, Algeria and Turkey, Egypt and Iran stand out as particularly notable cases.

Far from being a Western import, feminism in Egypt was indigenous. As historian Margot Badran bluntly puts it, 'The West is not the patrimonial home of feminism, from which all feminisms derive and against which they must be measured'. The written record of Egyptian feminists exists from the late-nineteenth century. Then, in 1909 writer Malak Hifni Nasif published *Al-Nisa'iyyat*, a compendium of works on women's rights, in Cairo, and in 1923 the Egyptian Feminist Union was formed, headed by activist Huda Sha'rawi. From a young age, Sha'rawi was acutely aware of the limitations her gender placed on her in society, such as keeping her from the education she craved. After observing a female poet who stayed with the family, Sha'rawi realised that 'with learning, women could be the equals of men, if not surpass them'.

Women's journals also started to be produced in Egypt in the early twentieth century. Nabawiya Musa, a *hafiza* (someone who has memorised the entire Qur'an) who decided to interpret the Qur'an for herself, published *The Magazine of the Young Woman* as well as a number of books focussing on the education and employment of women. It was the phenomenal, and very public, professional achievements of Nabawiya that set the precedent for the Egyptian government to award women 'equal pay for equal work' years later.

In 1945 the Arab Feminist Union was established and was based in Cairo with Huda Sha'rawi again at the helm. However, this movement was criticised by some of Sha'rawi's contemporaries for being nationalistic and elitist. Shortly thereafter, feminism in Egypt began to grow and change. Other women, such as philosopher and poet Doria Shafik and Fatma Reshad, led movements and activism, including storming parliament to demand rights for women and hunger strikes to gain women greater political participation in the 1950s, and the controversial text *Woman and Sex* by Nawal El Saadway was published in the 1970s.

Iranian Muslim women also have a rich tradition of struggling for gender equality. In the nineteenth century, Taherah Qurrat-ul 'Ayn, a learned theologian and public scholar, objected to all forms of the confinement of women and the establishment of distinct male and female gender roles. She is best known for her very public unveiling in 1848, which stunned her community. Her notable feminist contemporaries were women like Bibi Khanum Astarabadi, who declared 'all the problems and chaos faced in Iran and by its women were men's doings', and Taj-ul Sultanah, who 'criticized oppressive traditions and customs both for retarding Iran's development and for depriving women'.

In the twentieth century, women's publications in Iran began to flourish as they did in Egypt, with more than twenty separate women's periodicals in circulation by 1930. After the Islamic Revolution, feminism in Iran was split into secular and Islamic camps and, while the two didn't always agree, they proved they could work together on common projects for a shared goal. By the 1990s Islamic feminism—though not always referred to in such terms—was on the increase in the Muslim diaspora in the West.

It would be wrong, however, to suggest that there has always been a tension, much less a dichotomy, between Muslim women and feminism as such. Explicitly named feminism and feminists have existed in numerous Muslim countries for more than a hundred years, in both secular and religious forms. For quite some time, there have been Muslim women who operated outside a religious framework to fight sexism, and there have been Muslim women who use religion as one of the tools—in many instances, the only tool—in their struggle against the sexism around them. Some utilised the 'feminist' label and some did not. But all were engaged in challenging the sexism that they and their sisters faced.

The fight against sexism in the Muslim world is indigenous, and is an endeavour that sprang from the soil of Mecca and

Medina at the time of the Prophet Muhammad, and has now grown and spread throughout countless communities around the globe. It's also a fight that Muslim women have been carrying out for themselves, by themselves, against the very real injustices they experience in their varied communities, since the beginning of Islam more than 1400 years ago. Obviously not all Muslim women throughout history have had the means or the interest in fighting the sexism under which they lived, just as is the case for non-Muslim women. But it is simply incorrect to assume or argue that Muslim women have been entirely passive victims or, worse, active accomplices in their own oppression. As Roja Fazaeli, a scholar in Islamic civilisation, reminds us, while the term 'Islamic feminism' is recent, the act of Muslim women fighting sexism is nothing new.

Previous research supports using Islam as the primary way to challenge and even eradicate the sexist practices faced by many Muslim women, at least in some instances. It has even been suggested, for a challenge to sexism within Muslim communities to have any traction, it is imperative that it has theological backing. This is because to Muslims, as Asma Barlas says, 'theology matters', as 'it is one of the most powerful internal impulses for social critique and change in Muslim communities'. Roald confirms this fact when she states, 'Islam plays such a fundamental role in Muslim societies that for a social reformer to exclude Islam necessarily means failure. Many feminists, who previously struggled against female oppression in Western feminist terms have now adopted a more favourable attitude towards Islam.' The little field research done into the area also confirms this reality. In a comparative study of the way development agencies helping women operated in three Muslim majority countries (Sudan, Senegal and Malaysia), researchers found 'women activists in all three countries studied are increasingly confronted with the need to ensure the religious legitimacy of their agendas' (Nageeb, 2008). Religiously framed approaches have also been used to help prevent female circumcision in Indonesia and Malaysia and to improve education and employment prospects for women in Saudi Arabia.

Religion, though, should not always be considered as the ultimate response to all situations of sexism that Muslim women face. To do so ignores other very real contributing factors, such as poverty and political instability, which no amount of reinterpreting Qur'anic verses about women will address. Annie Bunting, an associate professor of Law at York University powerfully demonstrates this in her account of early marriages of Muslim girls in northern Nigeria. She investigated the way some Muslim leaders had proposed using *shariah* (divine religious law) to fight dangerous patriarchal practices occurring, such as marriage of underage girls and the lack of education of girls and women. Bunting highlights that while three authors attempted to systematically provide Islamic justification and requirement for educating girls and not marrying girls off before they were ready, they failed to achieve their goal because they were ultimately not tackling a solely religious problem. Indeed, by framing their approach in purely religious terms, their solution implied marriage of underage girls and lack of education for girls was a private, as opposed to a structural problem with no input required by the state. When one of the main factors in underage marriages and lack of education is poverty, as opposed to religious (mis)beliefs, a purely religious response that aims to educate women about their religious rights and men about their religious obligations as fathers and husbands will never succeed.

Bunting offers a telling example of this disjuncture with this excerpt from the 'Promoting Women's Rights Through Sharia in Northern Nigeria' report: 'Sharia makes it the duty of the father to provide maintenance and education for his children. In fact, Sharia insists that the father must pay for a nanny or domestic help to cater for his children where such services are needed.' Given poverty in Nigeria is staggeringly high at nearly 61 per cent, for the report to tell Nigerian Muslims that it is the religious obligation of men to pay for nannies and domestic help for their wives and children—even if there is religious basis for this—is, at best, unhelpful given that simply providing enough food for all family members can be difficult. Similarly, when the report addresses the issue of malnutrition it states:

> The refusal by some parents to make necessary provision for the proper development of their children is against the teachings of the *Sharia*. The Qur'an categorically and in the clearest expression possible commands that: ' … but he [the father] shall bear the cost of their feeding and clothing on equitable terms [2:233]'.

Implying that the malnutrition of children is due to fathers' sexist neglect of their religious duties as opposed to systemic poverty throughout the country not only blames men for something they have little control over, it also removes any responsibility from the state to improve the situation.

Bunting acknowledges that using Islamic sources as part of a response may be beneficial, however, especially when some traditional rulers in northern Nigeria try to dissuade poor people from accessing the state primary education system by telling them it is 'un-Islamic'. Thus, while a solution placed in a wholly Islamic framework is ill-conceived in certain circumstances, it should still be included as part of a whole-of-cause response. This is also relevant for misogynist practices that, while often discussed in religious contexts, actually have no religious motivation. This is the case of honour killings in Jordan, for example, where the perpetrators acknowledge quite openly that Islam forbids what they are doing, but insist that they need to do it regardless. In this situation, as in that of Bunting's discussion of northern Nigeria, a purely religious response to the issue would be ineffective.

Bunting's research provides significant insights for my own investigation, as it offers important contextualisation of the work of my participants. They are operating primarily in situations where systemic factors, such as poverty, are not the overarching cause of the experiences of Muslim women. Trying to gain better access to the mosque for women, providing domestic violence education in an Australian metropolitan city, and writing blogs about the depiction of Muslim women in pop culture, as my participants did for example, are not hampered by the same structural issues faced by Muslim women in other parts of the world. This is not to say that the work of my participants is not at least in part transferable to the situations of their sisters overseas, nor that other factors, such as racism, are not at play in the experiences of the women in my study, but that the experiences of my participants occur in a context in which religiously motivated sexism by other Muslims is a primary, not secondary, cause of their experiences.

While the root of sexism is patriarchy, sexism itself can be expressed in various ways in different societies and cultures. Some sexism is blatant, as when the unequal treatment of women is intentional and unambiguous. Other manifestations are subtler, and for that reason are often systemic or even pervasive. There are also hostile and benevolent forms of sexism and, as these two—especially benevolent sexism—have been linked to religiosity, it is appropriate to consider them further.

Peter Glick and Susan Fiske, both professors of psychology, first developed concepts of hostile and benevolent sexism in 1996:

> Hostile sexism is an adversarial view of gender relations in which women are perceived as seeking to control men, whether through sexuality or feminist ideology. Although benevolent sexism may sound oxymoronic, this term recognizes that some forms of sexism are, for the perpetrator,

subjectively benevolent, characterizing women as pure creatures who ought to be protected, supported and adored … This idealization of women simultaneously implies that they are weak and best suited for conventional gender roles; being put on a pedestal is confining, yet the man who places a woman there is likely to interpret this as cherishing, rather than restricting her (and many women may agree).

The connection between religiosity and an adherence to benevolent sexism has been established and it is worth considering whether the women in my study would subscribe to these beliefs, and thus possibly view some of their experiences not as sexism but as honouring practices. It is also plausible that there is overlap with this approach and the debate within Western feminism over 'equality versus difference'—that is, whether the goal for women should be equality (and thus arguably being identical) with men, or whether acknowledging and valuing the differences between men and women is a closer step to desired equity and justice.[4]

Such engagements with sexism can also be examined through the prism of Deniz Kandiyoti's (an academic specialising in gender relations) 'Patriarchal Bargain', which argues that everything women do takes place within the context of patriarchy, and women must negotiate patriarchy in all situations. Some women will choose to actively fight patriarchy, whereas others will be passive, or even defend patriarchy because they see the protection and respectability obtained under patriarchy as better, or at least more certain, than perhaps unobtainable rights and equality. But in all situations, patriarchy is the mediating force.

While I did not specifically ask my participants how they defined sexism and instead focussed on their self-described experiences of sexism, it is feasible that some may not view benevolent sexism as negative or even as sexism in our discussions on fighting sexism. They may instead view it through the terminology of the genders being 'complementary', as opposed to equal (a popular concept in many Muslim communities), and this should be kept in mind when reading their accounts. I do not state this in a condescending way. The idea of equality as it is understood in much academic literature is often based on Western, liberal ideas of freedom, rights and agency that do not always have currency in Muslim communities.

Given that my specific aim is to examine the ways that Muslim women living in the West fight sexism, it would seem natural to argue that this is, in fact, an investigation into Muslim/Islamic feminism. However, there are pockets of great resistance to the term 'feminism' in Muslim communities, which makes use of the term itself in my work problematic. 'Feminism' is seen as so alien and understood so negatively among many within Muslim communities, that it is like our very own 'f-word'. The reasons for this are many and multifaceted. The notion that Muslim women are helpless and hopeless is understandably offensive to Muslim women, as it smacks of arrogance, imperialism and condescension. As one frustrated Muslim woman doctor said to a surprised American journalist, 'These are our problems, not yours. We don't want anyone fighting for us—and we certainly don't want anybody feeling sorry for us (Kristof and WuDunn, 2009).'

This resistance to feminism should not be understood as a resistance to women's rights among Muslims, however. Muslims, by and large, are very enthusiastic to talk about 'Women's rights in Islam' when asked, and Muslim organisations have proudly run countless 'Women's rights in Islam' public lectures over the years; I have given some of these myself. Most of Muslims' resistance is specifically to feminism, which is often—wrongly, in my view—understood as inherently devaluing divinely mandated gender roles, the family unit and religion, and also has an uncomfortable history for many Muslims.

Much of the resistance to feminism relates to the history of Western involvement in Muslim countries. Feminism, for many, will always be irredeemably tainted by its association with colonialism and its perceived complicity in the breakdown of families. None of this is without basis. Historically, feminism, modernity and secularism—whether by external forces, or internal secular governments—were introduced as specific concepts at the same time in much of the Muslim world's history and are thus inextricably linked in the Muslim imagination.

Lila Abu-Lughod points out that, due to the Middle East's 'encounter with Europe, whether desired (as by reformers of the Ottoman Empire), ambivalent (for the Persian-speaking areas), or imposed through colonial occupation (for many in the Arab world)' at the end of the nineteenth and beginning of the twentieth centuries, there was 'intense preoccupation with women and family—not to mention with nation and society'. Arguments 'about redefining women's rights, clothing, and roles in and beyond the family' became vigorously discussed subjects for those interested in social reform. The disappointing progress of modernity in these societies, which often resulted in social inequality, meant that feminism as an idea was also seen as a failure, resulting in a strong reconsideration of the role Islam should play in personal and state life. There is also a linguistic component to the way feminism is seen as wholly Western and thus foreign. In Iran, for example, no Farsi word exists for feminism and thus, whenever the topic is discussed, the English word must be used.

In addition to being perceived as inherently Western and colonialist, feminism is also seen in much of the Muslim world as closely tied to secularism—generally understood to mean anti-religion—and thus Western feminists are viewed with a deep sense of wariness. As a result, some Muslim women who are currently engaged in the fight against sexism within a religious paradigm nonetheless dislike the term feminist. They argue that secular feminism in the West has failed to create an environment in which marriage and motherhood is acknowledged and respected, and that the work carried out in the home by women is devalued, which 'is one of the biggest grievances of Islamist women' (Maumoon, 1999). This is of special significance when we consider the great value many Muslim women—and most, if not all, Muslim societies in general—place on motherhood and marriage, coupled with the stereotypical view of Western feminism being anti-motherhood.

Ironically, such an understanding of Western feminism is as unfair and unfounded a caricature as the stereotypes so often made of Muslim women. Yet stereotypes and straw-men in both camps of Western feminists and Muslim women persist, jaundicing the ways one understands the other, and solidifying the belief that each side is both the victim of wilful misunderstanding and the possessor of fair appraisal and nuance.

Beyond mere semantics, some Muslims' negative attitudes towards feminism have a real impact. Muslim communities and leaders are often suspicious of agencies purporting to help women, even if run by locals, viewing them as Western, foreign, or non-Islamic, and as a continuation of colonisation. For example, faced with an internal, women-led push for tighter laws against honour killings in Jordan in 1999, the Secretary General of the Islamic Action Front, Abdul Latif Arabiat, called it 'a Western plot to destroy and corrupt our society … [the West] has occupied us militarily and politically, and now they want to destroy society, our last remaining fortress'.

It is clear the issue of women's empowerment in Muslim communities has an entrenched, decades long, and complicated political overlay. If it is not approached with the proper insights and sensitivities, it can in fact be counter-productive. Sometimes Western, and specifically American, aid projects that come in to Muslim societies to help women are perceived as part of a greater project of a 'War Against Islam'. The historically negative association of feminism with imperialism and paternalism that, as illustrated in the case of the Feminist Hawks, still exists helps explain why many Muslim communities throughout the world, including Western ones, disapprove of feminism. This perhaps also helps to explain why many Muslim women who are actively engaged in fighting sexism still refuse to embrace the term feminist.

Amina Wadud, one of the most effective and controversial Muslim scholar-activists of our time, and a participant in this research, wrote in 2006 that 'despite how others may categorize me … I still refuse to self-designate as feminist, even with "Muslim" put in front of it'. And this is despite conceding that her 'work is certainly feminist'. While she later went on to change her mind, her sentiment was not unique. Other Muslim women who fight sexism similarly eschew the description, even when they are essentially 'looking for a way to express much of what feminism at its base level in fact connotes' (Maumoon, 1999). I was therefore reluctant to use the word feminism in the questions I put to the women I interviewed, as I feared it may unnecessarily alienate them.

Feminism is simply a complicated term when used within a Muslim context. Beyond what has been discussed above, it has a delicate and often problematic political history for Muslims, because of its enforcement by both non-Muslim and secular authorities in Muslim lands. This tough, top-down approach to implementing a set of social policies aimed to address perceived gender inequality often had unpopular results that led to a subsequent rejection by many Muslims of anything even vaguely resembling feminism as a form of resistance to imperialism, whether by external Western forces or internal secular governments. Suddenly, a commitment to, or even an interest in, women's rights by Muslim women could be seen as treasonous and anti-Islamic because of the political history and climate in which people were operating.

In countries like Egypt, women's liberation was part of the Western colonial package. The Western colonial intervention in Egypt spoke openly of 'liberating Moslem [sic] women' (Van

Sommer and Zwemer, 1907). As mentioned earlier, Lord Cromer even made it an important focus of his time in that country. And in 1906, Western women missionaries held a conference on the perils of being a Muslim woman in Cairo. The proceedings of this conference were published in a text called 'Our Moslem [sic] Sisters: A cry of need from the lands of darkness interpreted by those who have heard it'. It says, 'Mohammedan law, custom, and the example of their founder place woman on a level with beasts of burden and no nation rises above the level of its women,' stating an opinion not out of place in modern sensationalist dailies. These concerned missionary women went on with all the passion of an angry tabloid columnist. 'And in looking at the millions of Moslems in the world to-day, and wondering why they are still as they were a thousand years ago, rather drifting backward than advancing, we turn to their women and find the cause.'

Such outsider attitudes occurred alongside Egypt's move into modernity. Because of modernity's association in the Middle East with colonisation and imperialism by the West, this coupling impacted on the way feminism (or things that resembled feminism) was received. And because modernity was viewed by many in Egypt as foreign and classist (it was Western and only benefitted the elite, most commonly men), its association with feminism meant women who even looked like they were operating within that system were viewed with suspicion. As feminist historian Margot Badran says, the 'uneven gendering of modernity and its implications cast deep shadows on women's modernist discourse', and this is particularly so for feminist discussions, which are considered Western, making them 'nationally subversive and treasonous'. This set up a dichotomy 'between Islam and modernity, constructed as an East–West antagonism'. And this situation has been ongoing 'in certain quarters in Middle Eastern societies but also by Westerners hostile toward or ignorant of Islam'.

This attitude is not entirely fair, of course, not least because the push for modernisation was not entirely external and Western. For example, Muhammad 'Abduh, an Islamic scholar and grand mufti of Egypt, arguably started the push for Egypt's modernisation through religious reform in the late 1800s. Similarly, indigenous feminist and women's rights movements have existed in Egypt for over a century, and expert scholarly opinion is that they certainly were not Western, as Badran puts it, 'no, feminism is not Western … Egyptian feminism is not French and it is not Western. It is Egyptian as its founders have attested and history makes clear.' And yet the belief of feminism's illegitimacy and foreignness within Muslim societies persisted, and continues to this day.

In other countries, such as Turkey and Iran, where there has not been Western colonisation, feminism has instead been imposed by the state, and yet was still seen as Western. For example, in Turkey in the 1920s, Kemal Ataturk built a secular nation-state from the ruins of the recently destroyed Ottoman Empire, and 'explicitly aligned modernization with Westernization, evacuating religion wholesale from his construction of modernity' (Badran, 2009). The state enforced removing the hijab and any prohibitions against women's education and work opportunities, yet it wasn't a feminist utopia. Independent women's movements were banned, the new privileges for women were really only accessible to (or preferred by) the elite, and many people felt displeasure with a forced abandonment of religious practices that had meaning for them, such as wearing religious attire, in the name of women's advancement.

Iran has a different experience of feminism, where women's rights were tied up in the revolution. Religious female role models like Fatima (the daughter of the Prophet Muhammad), an extremely important figure in Shia Islam (Iran is around 90 per cent Shia), were used as tools to create the political elite's archetypically preferred female character. So, during the Islamic revolution of 1979 Fatima was portrayed as a powerful, revolutionary female role model, but once the Islamic republic was established, the image of Fatima as the obedient wife and devoted mother became the prominent depiction, allowing the state to politically marginalise the women they had strongly relied on during the revolution. All of this occurred on the back of the Shah's modernisation of Iran, who used physical force to unveil women as part of his vision for the country, which was inspired by Kemal Ataturk. This enforcement, which angered and distressed many women who did not want to unveil[5] (and pushed them into lives of seclusion and limited education), made women's bodies among the many combat zones of the Iranian revolution. Iran now has a mix of what Roja Fazaeli calls secular feminists, Muslim feminists, Islamic state feminists, and Islamic non-state feminists, demonstrating Iranian feminisms are a fluid and contested terrain. Moreover, all of these groups have to operate under significant Iranian state pressure.

Such political histories of feminism/women's liberation/gender justice certainly linger in the memories of some Muslims when women's rights are brought up. This, coupled with the modern-day, near-constant assault about the treatment of Muslim women by those hostile to Islam, often from a feminist standpoint, makes the work of fighting sexism within the Muslim community difficult, and using the term feminism fraught.

In addition to politico–historical reasons, some Muslims also argue that feminism is itself un-Islamic. This springs from those problematic, stereotypical beliefs that feminism devalues women's domestic and motherhood roles, disputes religious practices and beliefs, and creates animosity between the sexes. Thus, when Muslim women (and sometimes men) work to eradicate sexism within Muslim communities, whether they use the title of feminist or not, they are often accused of being bad Muslims, fake Muslims, modernists (not said approvingly), hypocrites or as individuals who have been negatively influenced by external, Western forces.

Amina Wadud, in the introduction to her book *Inside the Gender Jihad*, spoke not only about this practice, but its ramifications as well. She says that as a Muslim women who fights 'for gender justice is Islam' she has been 'accused of working from outside Islam, doing whatever I want, but also rejected as anti-Islamic'. This means that if she and others like her wish to be 'accepted as truly Muslim, their struggles cannot go beyond established patriarchy or male authorities'. If they do 'they face the potential consequence of being labelled outsiders to Islam'. Wadud says there are many 'sincere women and men' who thus accept 'Islam as authoritatively defined by Muslim neo-conservative specialists or laypersons, sometimes erroneously called "fundamentalist",' which means they 'simply choose silence'.

These issues highlight why a number of Muslim women refuse the label 'feminist'. For some it is because of the negative history of the term within their cultural heritage, whether through its actual or perceived connection to colonialism and Western imperialism in countries like Egypt, or through state-imposed secular gendered policies in countries such as Turkey and Pahlavi Iran. Or it is due to a belief in the arguments of other Muslims who tell them feminism can only be external to authentic Islam, or because they know the term will have a negative impact on other Muslims' attitudes to their work and they reasonably want to minimise any controversy. It may also be from an awareness that while the term feminism wasn't first used until the 1880s in France, that Muslim women have been fighting against sexism within Muslim communities since the seventh century without needing the label. Thus, there is a tradition within Islamic history to do this work without such a tag. As Badran says, 'Some Muslim women describe the articulation and advocacy of a Qur'an-mandated gender equality and social justice as Islamic feminism. Others, however, do not', describing it as 'a woman-centred rereading of the Qur'an and other religious texts by scholar-activists'. She adds that 'the producers and users of Islamic feminist discourse include those who may or may not accept the Islamic feminist label or identity'.

For this reason, I was careful not to make my book simply about 'Islam and Feminism', as to do so necessarily precludes women who, for a variety of reasons, reject the label. It seems unnecessary to insist on a tag that some of the women I wanted to speak with did not adopt, even if others would insist that they are, in fact, feminist. This practice of working to eradicate sexism and of holding opinions that support the equal value and opportunity of men and women while at the same time rejecting the label of 'feminist' is what Patricia Misciagno called 'de facto feminism', and explains the discrepancy between the gains of the women's movement and the rejection of using the feminist label, even while there is pervasive support for feminism's goals.

The struggle to eradicate sexism from the lives of Muslim women, in theory and in practice, is extremely delicate. Its victories are hard won and often a long time in coming. It is understandable that some of these women would be reluctant to acquiesce to any description that may hinder the efficacy of their work. This is not to say, however, that there are not women in my pool of participants who would not proudly and publicly declare themselves Muslim feminists—indeed, many did. While these women take a faith-positive position, they are not dismissive of the ways in which Muslim women can face sexism from within their religious traditions and communities. In fact, they actively engage with these ways. They (and I) do not, however, see faith as inherently or inevitably sexist or problematic for women, and indeed, consider that it can be a powerful tool for both personal and social liberation, something that is often ignored or disdained by other feminist discourse.

Ultimately the label is not the point here—the women's stories and works are. While some of the references and even the women I interviewed use the terms feminism, Islamic feminism, Muslim feminism, etc., it is important to remember that such an expression is contested and not applicable for all of the women. It is important to note that not all Muslim women who fight sexism and misogyny do so within an Islamic paradigm. Indeed, a whole movement of Muslim women fight solely from a secular perspective. But when I talk about faith-positive feminism, I mean a feminism that perceives Islam as positive and useful in the task of fighting sexism, as opposed to benign or even damaging. And while the secular movement is still very active I have chosen to focus on women operating from a faith-positive stance that is rooted within the Islamic tradition for a number of reasons.

Firstly, it appears there has been something of a shift among Muslim feminists and Muslim women fighting sexism, towards a perspective more anchored in religion. I would think this is due to a number of factors, including feminism in the Muslim world going through its own waves, like other forms of feminism. In the Middle East, for example, Islamic feminism is slowly taking over from secular feminism because, as Badran observes, secular feminism, for all its achievements, seems to have run out of puff, offering few new ideologies or tools. It is also undoubtedly due to the growing recognition that any attempt to fight sexism against Muslim women that isn't grounded in theology is often rejected by the communities who sceptically view it as too Western, foreign or colonialist.

Additionally, in the last twenty-five years, there have been great gains made by female (and some male) theologians re-reading and re-interpreting the primary sacred sources, much of which was done out of frustration with the growing conservative approach to gender and a desire to respond to that. This created a space for Muslim women who want to fight misogyny to do so without feeling they had to see Islam as the cause. Indeed, many of them now argue that gender justice is an intrinsic part of authentic Islam and it is their obligation as committed Muslims to work towards this (Shaikh, 2003).

I am particularly interested in this exercise, as the general argument about the oppression of Muslim women is that they are oppressed because of Islam. For me, the great interest is how this fundamental notion is challenged.

Two
WITNESSES TO THEIR FAITH

> We need women doing everything. Because if we don't speak up, no one is going to give us our rights. We have to fight for them. We have to step up to the plate and work for them. Women have a different perspective and our perspective needs to be heard.
>
> — *Laleh*

All of the Muslim women I spoke to live in either North America or Australia. Muslim communities in these countries are highly culturally and ideologically diverse—in Australia alone, Muslims hail from more than 180 different countries. This is why academics most commonly refer to them as 'Muslim communities', rather than 'the Muslim community'.

In using the Muslim community, the invalid and inherently corrosive notion that Muslims belong to some ideological monolith, when great variance exists among those who subscribe to the faith, can be reinforced. I noticed particular variation of usage among my participants in this regard: some spoke of community—perhaps because of the strong religious emphasis on the *ummah*, the global Muslim community—others of communities. And many would use the two terms interchangeably, which

I feel is a good reflection of the way many Muslims perceive the *ummah*—at once seen as a unified body that is cohesive because of its shared beliefs, and yet also known to be incredibly diverse in all facets.

For consistency's sake, I have maintained the use of the word communities, as an acknowledgement of the real and significant difference among Muslims, and in order to avoid the problems posed by perceiving it as an undifferentiated mass. However, I do feel that doing so in some way negates the very real belief held by the majority of the women I spoke to who did not view the issue as either/or. There was fluidity in the way they understood the Muslim community/communities and their place within it/them, especially in a Western context.[1]

It may seem unusual or somehow restrictive to limit the geographic choice to Australia and North America, but it was a considered decision. While not the native home of Islam, Muslims have been in the West for centuries and are now growing in number and influence. Tariq Ramadan, a European scholar of Islam, states, 'We are currently living through a veritable silent revolution in Muslim communities in the West … This grassroots movement will soon exert considerable influence over worldwide Islam.' Homegrown Western Muslim scholars have considerable influence in Western Muslim communities, and this influence is starting to spread to the Middle East and beyond.

There has also been a significant increase in the number of Muslims living as minorities in non-Muslim countries, particularly in China and Western countries, and this increase is expected to continue. The Pew Forum projects an exponential growth of Muslims in North America, calculating the number in the United States to double over the next twenty years, to reach more than six million by 2030, and the number in Canada to almost triple by the same date, making them 6.6 per cent of the Canadian population. Similarly, in Australia 'the Muslim population is forecast to grow by nearly 80%, from approximately

399,000 to 714,000, while the non-Muslim population is projected to increase by roughly 18%' over the next two decades (Pew Forum, 2011). This projected growth is based on the current rapid growth of Muslims in North America and Australia over recent years; in Australia, the number of Muslims increased by 69 per cent between 2001 and 2011.

This increase is mainly due to immigration from Muslim-majority countries and a comparatively high birth rate compared to that of non-Muslims in the same country. I would therefore argue that rapidly growing Muslim communities living in Western countries with their own, legitimate scholars coupled with globalisation and increased internet access in Muslim-majority countries means that Western Islamic discourse is no longer just the poor cousin of 'real'—that is, Middle Eastern—Islam, but a genuine and important contributor to the global understanding and imagining of what Islam is and what it means to be Muslim.

When it comes to addressing sexism within Muslim communities, the contribution of Western Muslim women is of considerable significance, as one of the leading academics in the field of feminism in Islam and the Muslim world, historian Margot Badran, notes, 'Much of the innovative interpretive work, employing various feminist analytical techniques, is being published by Muslim women outside the Middle East'. However, as feminist historian Fereshteh Nouraie-Simone writes, this has been largely under-reported and unknown as 'Throughout the Muslim world, women are making their voices heard: documenting the realities of their own lives, exploring their changing identities, and insisting upon greater participation in the public sphere'. However, 'In the West, these dynamic realities have often been rendered invisible, or obscured by stereotyped representations of Muslim women'. Muslim women are 'too often seen as passive victims', even by Western feminists, 'rather than as agents who are actively engaged in efforts to reshape their individual selves, their cultures, and their societies. Islam is generally viewed, through Western eyes, as static, traditional, antimodern, and misogynistic'.

Not only is fighting sexism viewed as something that may take one outside the acceptable bounds of Islamic understanding, it is often viewed as foreign and colonial. According to Badran, fighting sexism or feminism is often seen by Muslims as just 'another form of Western assault upon their culture, and constituted a blasphemy to religion'. This is problematic, as Muslim women living in the West have made some of the most significant contributions to the field of re-reading sacred texts and primary sources from a female perspective available. Our increasingly globalised society means their contributions are now available to, and have considerable influence on, Muslims all over the world.

That Western countries have no state-run institutionalised religious authority also aids in the production of alternative, more woman-friendly renderings of Islam, as there is no singular voice—whether clerical or governmental—deciding what is a legitimate, genuine Islamic opinion, and what is heresy. While lay communities may resist or protest a certain approach, they cannot unequivocally stamp it out. The harsh censorship laws that exist in some Muslim countries in relation to open religious debate[2] also highlight the important work done by Muslim women living with greater freedom of speech and press in the West in this regard. Additionally, by focussing on Muslim women in diverse Western countries, my prospective participants offered greater opportunities to showcase the *ummah*'s racial, ethnic, national and cultural diversity than if I limited the range to just Muslim-majority countries.

Despite these issues, all the women I interviewed were actively involved in challenging sexism within Muslim communities in various ways: theologically, through grass-roots and more official forms of activism, online and in print. And for many of them, it was imperative to continue doing so. As Wadud confessed in her second book, 'I have lived inside the gender jihad long enough to know that I had to take it up. It was my only means to survive.'

I selected four categories of participants: theologians, activists, writers and bloggers. I felt this cast the net wide enough to capture significantly influential women who work in a variety of interconnected areas. These categories are broad enough to encompass the vastly different approaches that Muslim women are using to fight gender discrimination, while still being defined enough to allow for comparison and critique. These cannot, however, entirely be taken as stand-alone categories, for each relies on the other for validation and survival. Community activists, for example, would be completely ineffectual in challenging sexist treatment of women within marriage if they did not have the work of theologians to back up their claims, and the work of theologians would be practically useless if no one 'on the ground' was implementing their interpretations and ideas. The important interplay between scholarship and activism among Muslim women who work against sexism from within Islam means, as professor of religion Gisela Webb says, 'that any analysis or theory of women's nature, role, rights, or problems must include attention to the practical, immediate issues involved in actualizing the Qur'anic mandate of social justice and, concomitantly, that any considerations of "practical" solutions … must have sound theological grounding in the Qur'anic worldview.'

I began my search for participants by contacting those who were active in the areas of fighting sexism in various Muslim communities that I knew—either personally from observing their work first hand, or being exposed to their work through various media, such as books or websites. The rise of online sites, such as YouTube, blogs and tumblrs, has democratised who is considered a legitimate voice for Islam and has challenged some of the former gatekeepers to religious authority in Muslim communities. For this reason, it is unsurprising that young Muslim women would use it as a space to share ideas and connect with other like-minded women. The women I contacted would then sometimes suggest other women they felt I should also speak to, thus precipitating a snowball effect. It should be noted, however, that I did not ask my participants for additional names of people to contact; some just offered them. Only two of the women I contacted to request an interview declined or did not get back to me; all the rest agreed.

Twenty-three women participated in my research—sixteen are North American and seven are Australian. Fourteen were born and raised as Muslims, and the remaining nine are converts to Islam. Of these converts, three are African-American, five are Anglo, and one is Anglo-Iranian. The cultural backgrounds of the women who were born and raised as Muslim are diverse, and include India, Yemen, Egypt, Palestine, South Africa, Pakistan, Iraq, Bangladesh and Kashmir. All the women range in education levels from high school diplomas to doctorates. As a group, however, they are highly educated—all but one has a degree or else was studying to complete a degree. They range in age from twenty-one to over sixty.

Seven of the participants are single and never married, six are married (including one same-sex marriage), one is widowed, three are divorced and single, five are divorced and remarried, and one refused to answer. Eight of the women in my study have no children, seven are mothers and six are grandmothers. One participant is a stepmother (with no biological children), and one refused to answer whether she had children or not.

While these women may not be representative of all Muslim women—they may be more highly educated as a group than the average—they are representative of the type of Muslim women I wanted to profile: Muslim women who fight sexism within Muslim communities in Australia and North America. Some of these women have relatively low profiles, some are highly respected leaders within the Muslim community, and a small number are sometimes dismissed by various members of the Muslim community as provocateurs, sell outs, or fringe. However, all have engaged extensively in the work of fighting sexism within the Muslim community and utilised faith-based approaches to do so.

I was unwilling to only include very popular and esteemed women in my group of participants, as the history of the global women's rights movement is full of women both loved and loathed. While there were times when I disagreed with the approaches or political views of some of my participants, this work was never intended to be a list of 'my favourite people', but instead a collection of Muslim women engaged in the hard work of fighting sexism within the Muslim community from a religious framework. Universal acceptance, particularly in an area as charged as this, could never be a criterion.

Some women were adamant that their real names be attached to their words and stories, and some were equally resolute that their identity be completely protected—pseudonyms are marked with an asterisk. In gathering these stories, I wanted the women to be honest and unhindered. That's why I did these interviews with the offer of anonymity. Not everyone accepted this offer. Some insisted their names be made public—they wanted their name attached to all their quotes, as part of what they viewed as an authentic commitment to Muslim women's rights, voices and experiences. Others, though, were equally insistent to be protected from any form of identification before agreeing to speak with me.

There was a notable cultural difference in who was prepared to be named and who was not: twelve of the sixteen North American women wanted to be named, and only four did not. Of the four who did not, it was for reasons of employment confidentiality (such as the woman who worked for the American armed services) or for safety and privacy reasons (such as the woman who was a survivor of domestic violence and didn't want her answers to be connected to her ex-husband). Whereas every

Australian participant asked to be given a pseudonym. There was a genuine concern among all the Australian women I interviewed that other Muslims would discover what they had said, and that this would have a damaging impact on their professional reputations for continued community work, or invite criticism. These women seemed very concerned that speaking too frankly about the challenges they faced fighting sexism within Muslim communities would attract the criticism of their co-religionists. This demonstrated communities feeling under intense scrutiny and even siege by outsiders, and that exposing internal problems was strongly frowned upon by insiders.

I was acutely aware of the trust the women with whom I spoke placed in me. As the conversations with the women progressed, I became aware that the candid ways in which the women spoke to me, because of that trust, could inadvertently lead to harm and criticism of the women and the communities they valued. I felt a burden, as I knew to publicise some of the things Muslim women had openly told me could be used to reinforce negative opinions about Islam, Muslims, and particularly Muslim women. Yet, to whitewash it seemed dishonest to my sisterhood, and also condescending, as it assumed the women with whom I spoke had no awareness of these ramifications, and needed me to protect them. Calculating exactly what form my solidarity would take in conveying their stories was a delicate issue to negotiate, and one I continue to struggle with. Whatever their reasons, and whatever their decision, I wanted to make sure they were in control. I was interviewing Muslim women on matters I knew to be delicate and socially flammable. As sociologist Janet Finch says, that is, after all, the job of the sociologist, especially the feminist sociologist who shares the typically powerless position of the people they research.

What follows is a brief biography and description of the demeanour of the women in their interviews with me. In these summaries I include some brief comment on their personalities, because I wanted to depict my participants beyond mere demographical data and remind the reader that these are real women living real lives. My interview questions were designed to encourage the women to share their experiences and provide as many examples to illustrate their experiences as possible. For this reason, I would often say to them, 'Can you tell me a story to illustrate when that happened?' This is because I was eager to record, not just the facts of their lives, but also the musicality— the lived realities, the exciting moments of realisation, the turning points, the achievements and crushing disappointments.

Adrienne*

Adrienne defines herself as a doctor and activist. She is a founding member of Muslims for Equality and Human Rights (MEHR), an organisation that promotes women's and LGBTQ rights for Muslims in Montreal.

Adrienne spoke eloquently of her tireless struggle to create equality (as opposed to equity) for Muslim women within Muslim communities, saying, 'Some [Canadian Muslims] are really working towards an actual equity. Even though I think equity is no better than inequality, they are trying to make their patriarchal experience as fair to women as possible. The equality fight is harder. I gave the *adhan* [call to prayer] recently at a mosque. I was invited to do it. Even though this is perfectly [religiously] legal, someone told me there were men shaking their heads. They belong to this liberal mosque and they are shaking their heads. Uphill battle.'

Adrienne is a French-Canadian convert to Islam and is partnered with three small stepchildren. Intelligent and open, she is in her late thirties.

Amina Wadud

Arguably the most well-known activist and theologian for Muslim women's rights in the English-speaking world, Amina is a grandmother and African-American convert to Islam. She penned the text that opened the gates for numerous other feminist critiques of Islamic theology, *Qur'an and Woman: Rereading the sacred text from a woman's perspective*, her 1993 book that started life as her PhD dissertation. She has written other important publications since then, such as *Inside the Gender Jihad* in 2006, but none has been as groundbreaking as *Qur'an and Woman*. Since then she has engaged in other notable events, such as leading the (in)famous female-led prayer in New York in 2005.

She defines herself as a theologian who is an activist, telling me she was initially just a scholar because it was non-confrontational, but soon came to realise that 'A theory is only as good as your ability to put it into practice'. However, she says, 'I don't put them at the same level. I think I still give primacy to knowledge production. But I can't give up putting these things into implementation. It is necessary to challenge stasis in thinking and acting, and the challenge in the thinking is what holds us back as an ummah, I believe, so my priority is still in the area of knowledge production.'

Fiercely intelligent and humorous, Amina is a pioneer in every sense of the world.

Asifa Quraishi-Landes

Asifa is an Assistant Professor of Law at the University of Wisconsin. Asifa told me she was 'not specifically interested in women's issues or women's rights. I never studied feminism. But if you are a Muslim woman who knows anything about law, you are naturally going to be asked about women's issues in Islam. I would be asked to participate on panels and it was always on women's rights instead of law, which frustrated me. So just by necessity, to be able to answer these questions properly, I began to research some areas of Islamic law that had impacted women.'

Her research led to some profoundly important texts being written, most notably *Her Honor: An Islamic critique of the rape laws of Pakistan from a woman-sensitive perspective* in 1997, and *What if Shariah weren't the Enemy? Rethinking international women's rights advocacy on Islamic law* in 2011. Such works, she told me 'are being used in reform in a legal sense', which is highly significant and could potentially lead to lives being saved. However, she went on to tell me that such endeavours are a small part of her overall work.

She is a charming mix of professional but affable. Of her parents, she says, 'My mom is white and my dad is Indian, and both parents were real activists.' She lives in the United States with her husband and children.

Asra Nomani

Asra is a single mother to one son who is also a writer, journalist and 'accidental activist'. An engaging mix of languid and inquisitive, she was born in India and moved to the United States when she was four. A former *Wall Street Journal* correspondent, she didn't write about Islam or Muslims for a long time into her writing career, saying: 'I had been writing for twenty years ... but never wrote about it or researched it. For someone who's intellectually curious, I had never pursued it. I realised that I had been asleep for all those years as a writer. It had to become personal to wake me up.'

Asra defined her baby's conception (when she was unmarried; something generally frowned upon in Muslim communities) and the murder of her friend, journalist Daniel Pearl, by an al-Qaeda member in Pakistan as the impetus that changed things for her. Her activism for Muslim women includes penning 'The Islamic Bill of Rights for Women in the Mosque' and 'The Islamic Bill of Rights for Women in the Bedroom', and being a lead organiser of the female-led *jummah* [congregational prayers held at the mosque every Friday] prayer in New York in 2005 that received worldwide attention. She also wrote *Standing Alone in Mecca: An American woman's struggle for the soul of Islam* in 2006 about her experiences as a single mother in a Muslim community (and its connection to Islamic matriarchs) and it also chronicles her experiences of trying to gain greater access to the mosque and subsequent activism.

Asma Barlas

Fiercely intelligent and thoughtful, Asma was originally born in Pakistan and now resides in America. She is a professor of politics who has a special interest in the way women create and understand theological knowledge, and wrote extensively about it in her 2002 text 'Believing Women' in *Islam: Unreading patriarchal interpretations of the Qur'an*. Instead of having a narrow focus on women's rights, she states that 'what most influences my work is my understanding of a just God who does not transgress against the rights of anyone (do *zulm* [oppression]); for me, that is the point of departure for contesting the abuse and oppression of women in the name of Islam.'

Despite receiving some criticism for her work, Asma, who is in her sixties, remained unperturbed, and said in her interview with me, 'Quite frankly, I don't do the work that I do because I am encouraged or discouraged by this or that person. I do it as a witness to my own faith.'

Asma Uddin

Asma was born in Miami to parents who were originally from Pakistan. A qualified lawyer, she defines herself primarily as an activist. Asma started the acclaimed and popular blog AltMuslimah (Muslimah being the feminine version of Muslim)—which uses analysis and personal narrative from a variety of writers to tackle numerous aspects relating to gender in Islam—after experiencing inner turmoil about what it meant to be a Muslim woman in college, and realising she was not the only one. She told me of the struggle she went through at university as her happily naive understanding of Islam came head-to-head with some disturbingly sexist beliefs and practices of the other Muslim students.

After three years of university and increasing inner tension over what her faith actually taught about women, the 9/11 terrorist attacks happened, causing even greater reflection. She told me that it led her 'to believe that it just couldn't be, that there couldn't be gender inequality in Islam. We couldn't have been created like that. This process was really agonising—my entire four years of college was spent on this and I realised that I was not the only one to go through this, so I started a book club and discussion group to discuss gender issues [in Islam]. And that's what triggered [starting AltMuslimah]—tonnes of women are going through this, there's a need for a forum and there's no forum ... I felt like I went through my struggles for a reason.'

Pregnant with her second child when I interviewed her, Asma is mild-mannered and astute. She lives in Washington DC with her husband and children.

Ayesha Mattu

Ayesha was born in Pakistan and has lived most of her life in the United States. She is an author who edited the controversial 2002 *Love, InshaAllah* anthology, a compilation of true stories from a variety of Muslim women about their experiences with sexual (as opposed to familial) love. The book was divisive as it included accounts by same-sex attracted women and women who had had sexual relationships outside of marriage (both of which are traditionally seen as unacceptable in Islam), and while she wasn't deliberately courting controversy, Ayesha actively wanted 'orthodox and secular women in a single volume'.

Ayesha was clear that her book 'is not a dating manual nor is it an Islamic book—it's just a reflection of the lived experiences of American Muslim women [because] I loved the idea of amplifying women's voices to tell their own stories. It's not about waiting for someone to let us speak but creating our own space and telling our own stories.'

Ayesha has a serene yet steely persona, and is married with one child. She is aged in her forties.

Daisy Khan

Daisy was born in Kashmir and describes the first sixteen years of her life there as one of interfaith tolerance and respect. She now resides in New York, and is the executive director at the American Society for Muslim Advancement (ASMA). It is through ASMA that Daisy began the Women's Islamic Initiative into Spirituality and Equality (WIISE), which is designed to empower Muslim women all over the world through different channels, such as the 'Jihad to end violence' campaign and the world's first global woman's *shurah* (consultation) council.

During our interview she told me about how she came to this line of work (having previously been an architect), saying, 'I studied other women's movements, and realised they were all the same—women are always written out of histories. So we are creating a modern-day suffrage movement for Muslim women that is global and ageless.' A lovely mix of business-like and spiritual, she is married with children.

Ghayda*

Ghayda has a Yemeni background and lives in the United States. A published author, she is in her late twenties, energetic and curious. She began the well-known Muslim women's website Beyond the Veil that critically addressed anything relating to Islam and the female gender in 2007, as she 'felt marginalised and needed an outlet'. The site was one of the first and most widely known blogs that engaged such issues in the English language and often in an openly feminist way. The site and its team of writers (who Ghayda oversaw) were frank and fearless in its analysis, even engaging with potentially explosive issues, such as homosexuality and domestic violence. After a few years, Ghayda had to stop managing the site, as despite the many hours she devoted to it, it was a voluntary position and this was not financially viable for her. She passed the management of the site on to another Muslim woman and it continues to be prolific and widely read.

Hakimah*

Hakimah is a US army colonel in her early forties and was born in Bangladesh. Her work in the armed services started after 9/11, when she felt compelled to help her country. The army utilised her repeatedly in cultural engagement with Muslims when she was deployed overseas, and this work has given her many opportunities to directly engage with Muslim women around the world.

When engaging with Muslim communities overseas while stationed in their countries, her attitude to activism with Muslim women fighting sexism is pragmatic. She says, 'We need to focus on the literacy part. Are women reading the texts for themselves? Do they have the capacity to read what the thing says for themselves? If we do not give her the fundamental right to read it for herself, nothing will change. Reading Qur'an in Arabic is important, but in terms of comprehension they must read it in terms they understand.'

Hakimah is direct, uncompromising and incredibly hard working. She is single with no children.

Ify Okoye

Ify is warm and engaging and in her late twenties. She is a nursing student, and considers herself a blogger and activist. She has done a lot of her activism work in the area of Muslim women's access to the mosque. On the 'about' section of her blog, she includes a large photograph of her and other Muslim women praying, a group of uncertain-looking police officers standing behind them, with a caption that reads, 'My friends and I praying on the sidewalk outside the Islamic Center of Washington after risking arrest for praying in the main hall.'

Ify discussed this and other experiences in our interview in a hotel lobby in Washington DC. She told me that after this event, she was 'officially banned' from the mosque because she refused to pray in the women's section, saying that, for the men who called the police on her, 'it's all about authority and control'. Her writing has often focussed on the area of women's access to the mosque, including the post 'The Penalty Box: Muslim women's prayer space', which generated nearly four hundred comments on the popular website Muslim Matters.

She was once a regular writer for Muslim Matters but told me during our interview that she had been kicked off the writing team, saying there was too much conflict between her attitudes towards women's access to the mosque and the general belief of the managing board of the website. She said this was good for her as being on Muslim Matters and being mindful of their sensibilities was 'hindering in a tremendous way', and that solely writing on her own blog gave her 'more freedom and more empowerment'.

Ify is married and converted to Islam in her late teens. She describes herself on her blog as 'AfriYorkan (part African, part New Yorker, fully American)'; she was born in New York to Nigerian parents.

Ingrid Mattson

The Chair of Islamic studies at a Canadian university, Ingrid Mattson converted to Islam in her twenties while doing relief work in Pakistan. While she doesn't consider herself as primarily interested in women's issues, she has made a significant contribution for Muslim women, the most notable being her election as the first female president of the Islamic Society of North America (ISNA), the largest peak body of Muslims in the United States.

She has also written articles on Muslim women and their rights, such as female leadership in Islam. However, she firmly states that she doesn't 'see myself as someone who is primarily interested in women's issues. I'm interested in the whole community, in helping our community fulfil its responsibilities and engage in society. And of course if there are obstacles to women doing that, I've pointed that out or advocated for changes, but I'm not a gender leader; that's not my primary area of focus. But when it needs to be addressed, I'll address it. People assume that I'm interested in gender stuff just because I'm a woman.'

Unflappable and erudite, she is a married mother of two.

Jessica*

Aged in her late twenties and a Canadian convert to Islam, Jessica is the editor of the blog started by Ghayda. She is easy-going and circumspect. Jessica described to me the process of becoming the new editor as something she 'just fell into', saying 'I'm interested in the issues the blog discusses and so I sent a sample of my writing and it went from there'.

She saw her blogging as an important expression of her ethos, saying, 'For us to be able to say what we're saying through our actions as well as our words. As Muslim women critiquing society, there's a value in us being there as Muslim women who are outspoken and have opinions. In doing that, we challenge stereotypes. Through our actions we try to make the same points we make in our writing. My goal is to put a different perspective of who Muslim women are out there.'

Jessica is a masters student who spends an equal amount of time editing her website as she does on her studies, and is single with no children.

Karima*

Gentle and reserved, Karima is a respected professor of anthropology at an Australian university, and a former accountant. She converted to Islam in her twenties while studying in Morocco, and is now a grandmother. As an expert in the area of women in various Muslim societies, she is often called on for public comment.

Despite her engagement in many local community initiatives for Muslim women over quite a number of years, she sees herself primarily as an academic. In our interview, Karima raised some of the initial struggles she had as a Muslim woman within her Muslim community, saying, 'When I became a Muslim there were things I found difficult for women, particularly at the mosque. Men would rush out and welcome my husband and son and then they'd just say to me, "Women's door—up the back." I found that very irritating. I wouldn't describe myself as a radical feminist but I do have feminist leanings. And I did before becoming Muslim. I try to work quietly, however.'

Karima was a pioneer in working with some of the first organisations set up in Brisbane, Australia, by Muslim women, for Muslim women, with the express purpose of serving and empowering their constituents.

Laleh Baktiar

Laleh is a psychologist and author with an outgoing and entertaining personality—I laughed many times while interviewing her. She is also an Iranian-American convert to Islam and wrote what is believed to be the first English translation of the Qur'an that used 'inclusive language' (her words), called *The Sublime Quran*, published in 2007. In doing so, she translated terms by referring to other places in the Qur'an where the same word or term was used, which she said provided 'consistency and internal reliability'. She also consciously tried to take a female-friendly approach or incorporate the female perspective, especially on verses that had previously been translated or understood to be problematic for women, such as verse 4:34, which is sometimes understood to mean a husband can beat his wife.

Of tackling this verse, in particular, Laleh called it 'a remarkable period of research', and went on to discuss how her studies into the Arabic lexicon and other uses of the term *daraba* (the key term in the verse) in Arabic, plus investigation into the *sunnah* (the way of the Prophet Muhammad) led her to truly believe the correct understanding of that term was 'go away from', and not 'beat', as had previously been understood.

She has written twenty books, and completed her masters by the age of fifty-five, when she was a divorced grandmother. She said that since she published her translation of the Qur'an, she 'has been much more active in the area of women's rights, especially in the area of domestic violence'.

Latifa*

Now a grandmother of eight, Latifa converted to Islam in her twenties and went on to marry and have four children. She is very much an activist, and is lively and always involved in various Muslim community initiatives and new personal ventures—she has just embarked on her fourth degree. She established one of the first centres for Muslim women in Adelaide, but said she got very little support from the local Muslim community because, she believed, she was a convert without backing from an ethnic community.

Like Karima, Latifa was a pioneer in many ways, opening the first Islamic childcare and afterschool care centre in Adelaide but this also earned her a lot of backlash. She spoke candidly of feeling quite lonely in her journey.

Malika*

Aged in her early thirties, Malika lives in Australia and is of Pakistani descent. She considers herself an activist and describes her path as 'growing up in community work', specifically focussing on the rights of women. She recently established a successful

Muslim women's organisation with a focus on policy and teaching Muslim women their social and religious rights.

Very humble and self-effacing despite her achievements in a number of areas, Malika still spoke with frustration at other Muslim women's lack of self-belief, about the way women are reluctant to be leaders, saying, 'The most common response I get from women when I ask them to get involved is that "I'm not good enough" or "I don't want to get involved with the politics". They are happy to work behind the scenes but don't want to be up the front. Men are more inclined to say yes to opportunities to lead unlike women. Men are not questioned about being leaders the way women are, and men seem to have a sense of entitlement about being leaders.'

Malika has a university education and is single.

Nahida Nisa

Aged in her early twenties and studying at university, Nahida manages the website The Fatal Feminist. She is quick to tell me she 'dislikes the term blogger', and that she doesn't 'consider blogging activism'. She thinks of herself as a writer, at least in part because of her website, which she has managed since 2011. She describes the blog as, 'a declaration of jihad on the cultural oppression of Muslim women'. It is a site with a combination of posts from Nahida and guest posters who engage with various matters of sexism within Islamic practice or the Muslim community.

Nahida told me her greatest challenge in her work is to 'get rationality through patriarchy's thick, prideful skull, and the thick, prideful skull of patriarchal men'. Frank and fearless, she is single and has no children, and also teaches feminist Qur'anic interpretation, which she feels is the closest thing to activism that she does.

Sarah*

Sarah is a forthright, passionate young woman in her early twenties who writes a tumblr entitled Bad Ass Muslimahs. When she describes the point of her tumblr, she says 'I've had enough of the sensationalist, exoticised, demeaning portrayals of Muslim women seen all throughout the media, and this is my way of countering all the nonsense. This is not an attempt at "breaking stereotypes" or trying to enlighten people, if you're ignorant enough to believe that Muslim women are oppressed and subjugated by Islam then that's your own problem. This is my way of giving recognition to all the women who inspire me, and hopefully sending out some positive vibes.'

The tumblr profiles Muslim women from a variety of backgrounds who are successfully engaged in various activities and pursuits, which is a stark contrast to the one-dimensional victim of many media portrayals of Muslim women. Sarah stated that one of the main reasons she started the blog was because she was sick of the way 'white feminists and Muslim men' spoke about Muslim women, declaring, 'We need to speak for ourselves'.

In our interview Sarah was careful to say that she does not consider herself a Muslim community representative or spokesperson: 'I don't try to speak on behalf of all Muslim women, I try to show diversity on my blog, but I don't try to say "this is what all Muslim women are like". It really bothers me—this idea that if you're part of a minority, you have to be "representative". Everyone needs to try to get their voice in if they can.'

Sarah is a university student and also part of a Muslim women's writing group that she has helped to compile some anthologies and publish books of poetry. Her family is originally from Palestine and she came to Australia when she was two years old.

Tayyibah Taylor

Tayyibah was born in Trinidad and moved to Canada with her family as a young girl. She told me about the profound experience of picking up a magazine by and for black people and finally seeing people of colour portrayed positively in the media, and wanting to create something similar for Muslim women, especially those who wear the hijab. This desire led to the creation of the award-winning flagship *Azizah* magazine. She edited this until her death in 2014, after our interview.

Ultimately, *Azizah* was by and for Muslim women, and not about trying to address stereotypes that non-Muslims had. As Tayyibah told me, 'Remember that *Azizah* was a pre-September 11 magazine, so I didn't start it to challenge that. I didn't start it to change perceptions outside our community although it is something that has happened. My motivation was to give voice to Muslim women's stories.'

Warm, generous and confident, Tayyibah was a convert to Islam and a grandmother. Not long after our interview, when Tayyibah passed away from cancer, there was a large outpouring of grief online and in American Muslim communities, a testament to how much she was valued.

Umaymah*

Umaymah lives in Perth, Australia, with her husband and two children, and is of South African background. She considers herself an activist who has been doing various forms of community activism work, especially around Muslim women's rights, for more than a decade. She has sat on, and chaired, the board of numerous Muslim women's organisations, including those that specifically focus on women's rights in a welfare capacity.

She was open about some of the structural sexism she faces in her local Muslim community, such as access to the mosque, when I interviewed her, saying, 'I don't always feel welcome.

It's frustrating to always be told to use the back entrance, behind the car park. It's like, why bother? It seems pointless. I want to use the main entrance, which is beautiful. I don't look at the mosques as a centre for the community; mosque committees are invariably, 99 per cent, run by men, who even if they try to represent women still don't get it. I can only do so much … I don't have the energy to change it.'

Calmly confident, she is in her forties and recently obtained her master's degree.

Waajida*

Waajida was born in Egypt and came to Australia as a young child. She is aged in her early forties and sees herself as an activist. An active community worker, she has been engaged in this line of work around Muslim women since her teens. She is a regular teacher of Islamic classes to women, heads a Muslim women's organisation, called Amani Services in Sydney, and also does a lot of counselling for Muslim women in areas such as domestic violence and spiritual growth.

Her work has been challenging, and she spoke to me with frustration about the lack of support for Muslim women leaders and the sense of responsibility she has for Muslim women. She says, 'Women just aren't supported, like—why would a woman go through all this? Sometimes I stop and think, "Why am I still in it after all these years?" It would be easier just to take care of my children and continue on with my studies and do what I want to do. But then I look at all the women who come to my classes and I think, "Who is going to advocate for them?" So I can't stop, I just can't.'

Waajida is gentle and attentive, and a married mother to four children.

Zafreen*

Zafreen is an intelligent and outspoken award-winning film-maker, and an activist. She has directed numerous short films and documentaries for children and young people, including a number of narratives with Muslim protagonists. She is a frequent media contributor and, in our discussion, raised her frustration at the lack of practising Muslim women who engage with the media, saying she is 'frustrated that so many Muslim women who are committed to their faith and are religious and want to be an activist don't see media contribution as important. That's frustrating that they're apathetic.'

She lives in Melbourne, Australia with her husband and three young children, and her family is originally from Iraq.

When interviewing my participants, my aim was to dig deep into their lives, to sift through the layers of their different experiences and thoughts and highlight aspects of their realities that weren't always shared or known. This was not for novelty's sake but because I was operating within a legacy in which too many Muslim women's stories had been buried, with the earliest accounts scant and the modern-day accounts minimal. The urgency of this was brought home to me during my research in the most tragic way.

Towards the end of my work, one of the women I interviewed died. While I was in the final stages of editing this book, another woman I interviewed also died. I feel an extra level of responsibility to share their stories, and also have become acutely aware of how easy it would be for their stories and stories similar to theirs to vanish. Telling their stories isn't just about these inspiring women, it's also for them.

Three
JOURNEY TO THE FIGHT

> Women contributing to this area will restore to women the power given to us by God that men have fearfully stolen from us; it's reclamation, and it's an invaluable right. For women to contribute to interpreting religious texts is a religious practice—the practice of jihad.
>
> — *Nahida*

Ify is a woman who takes her faith seriously. She has written articles about Islam for one of the most widely read English-language Muslim websites in the world, she wears the hijab, and she prays her required prayers. She is also someone who cannot accept injustice, and what she believed was happening at her local Washington DC mosque was injustice.

When Ify went to pray there she found they had chained the door to the women's section shut from the inside. If a fire broke out, there would be no way for the women to escape. She contacted the mosque board to raise her concerns, but they ignored her. Frustrated with the way this mosque shunted women into a secluded space for prayer, Ify and her female friends decided to pray in the men's section, still behind the men, as a form of peaceful protest. She called them 'pray-ins'. The mosque committee was so enraged they called the police on the group for trespassing. Calling her a 'troublemaker' and a 'rebellious women', they banned Ify from the mosque.

What prompts Muslim women to fight sexism in their communities? Do they have strong female role models who inspired them? Did they feel their religion was contributing to the struggles they faced as women? Were they motivated by a desire to make Islam look better to outsiders? My conversations with the women showed, perhaps surprisingly, it was none of these. Instead they indicated that their journeys originated from places of pain, from desires to see remarkable Muslim women in the spotlight and an unwavering belief in the role their faith could and should place on improving the situation for Muslim women.

Despite the range of women I interviewed, it was clear there were four consistent motivators behind why they pushed back against the sexism they faced:

- dissatisfaction with Muslim—or purported Islamic—attitudes towards women

- strong personal history of fighting injustice

- period of difficulty that led to them investigating their faith's approach to women more deeply

- desire to have Muslim women's voices amplified.

While in many respects discrete, these driving forces also overlapped at times, with each woman identifying at least one rationale, and some naming more than one. The categories are interdependent, and the women drifted between them depending on the stage of their lives and the issue being addressed.

Waajida gave a long, thoughtful and, at times, emotional response when I asked her about Muslims' responses to her work of fighting sexism as a teacher and community worker in Sydney. Her long narrative also illustrates the multifaceted nature of this issue for many of the women I spoke with, as Waajida's story showed she experienced all four motivations.

Waajida, a mother of three boys and one girl, began as a leader for young Muslim girls when she was a teenager, encouraged into the role by a male religious teacher. She reflected on how natural it felt to her to work exclusively with women, and how combative experiences working with men, including her male teacher, had reinforced her desire to work solely with females. However, only working with women was something that troubled Waajida. She acknowledged it wasn't holistic to exclude men from her organisation in Western Sydney, but lamented, 'I cannot find the kind of men out there that are willing to sit on a table and respectfully negotiate and discuss and feel the plight of women the way women feel them. I've yet to find that. And if I do find that, they'll be the first men on my team.'

I asked Waajida how Muslims responded to her challenging the other, sexist interpretations of Islam to which her female students had been exposed, and who was encouraging of her work. She only got a couple of sentences into her answer before she began to cry.

'Ever since I began working with the Islamic Outreach Foundation, which is a mixed [male and female] organisation, I've always felt that whatever I said was looked upon as if I was a feminist,' she bitterly noted. 'And the "feminist" word is a dirty word in the Muslim community, and probably in the wider community. In the Muslim community it's just *haram* [forbidden], it's just wrong. I was called Margaret Thatcher growing up.'

I asked Waajida to clarify why people called her Margaret Thatcher, of all things. 'I was opinionated,' she mused. 'Margaret Thatcher was known as the lady with the iron fist. It was so basic and yet they saw that as radical. Things like when we sat in classrooms, I'd prefer the women sat beside the men, not behind the men. [I wanted] women presenting at programs, not just the men. [I wanted] female teachers teaching the men, not just teaching the women. That was seen as radical, and it probably still is seen as radical today.'

At this point, Waajida realised that in two decades of work as a leader and teacher of Muslim women and girls, she had not found an imam she could work with as a partner. 'It's only now that I'm seeing men that are married to these women that I'm working with that are likeminded and I'm like, "Wow, there are men out there [who see us as equals]. They're young, but they are out there!"'

So how did this happen? 'Perhaps,' she says, 'there has always been a group of men who think this way but they've never had an opportunity to even voice their opinion. Maybe there are a lot of men who think the way the Muslim community treats women is just wrong, but they think, "If I speak out, what will other men think of me?"'

Waajida found a paradoxical reaction to her work within Australian Muslim communities: they loved the egalitarian message of Islam she taught non-Muslims in her speeches, but were sharply resistant to any change in community behaviour she suggested. Muslims 'are not interested in actual change,' she told me. 'When I do the kind of work that I do, the Muslim community treats me in two different ways: They love me, because I can speak to non-Muslims. They go "*mashaAllah mashaAllah*". But when I work in terms of real change in the Muslim community, it's "No, no, no, no good".'

She added, 'They don't want change, everyone's happy. Especially the men who hold the seats. Why wouldn't you be happy on your big throne? They've been taught that men are superior. I don't care what anyone says, they have been taught that, in our mosques they've been taught that. Even the imams when they speak about it, they don't believe it. It's just nice words. Because if they believed in it, they'd be advocating against domestic violence, they'd be setting up programs. It's just nice words to show the West, "Look, look. We have equality."'

Here is a crucial difficulty for the women I interviewed: there appears to be, at least for many of them, a knee-jerk resistance to their work within the Muslim community, simply because they are women. Waajida acknowledged this when I asked if she felt she would be treated differently if she were a man: 'That would be well received. That would be so different. My gender plays a big part.' Waajida also acknowledged, however, that her work might only bear fruit for future generations, saying, '*InshaAllah* [God willing] I do not pass away from this world until I see a real a change. And if I do, then *inshaAllah* the change will still happen, so long as I have planted that seed. We need to have change, we can't keep going this way.'

So, why does Waajida persist with her work? She said it is because she firmly believes women have a different contribution than men to make to society. 'I strongly believe we operate from a heart perspective, what we have to offer is totally different to what men have to offer. I'm not a man-basher! But society needs what women have to offer.'

As she was speaking, Waajida realised her motivation was more essential than mere gender balance. She said, 'On a basic level, the first thing that comes to my mind when you ask the question is: because we exist. We have a right. We are human beings. Allah created us, we worship Allah and our love for the *deen* [way, religion] just makes us come out and serve. I don't know how to live life without contributing. It doesn't even enter my thinking. Because I exist. Because I breathe, therefore I work.'

I asked Waajida where her women's rights perspective came from. She told me about growing up in a home where her mother was abused and women were disrespected, belittled and sexualised. This element of sexualisation was particularly troubling for Waajida: 'I grew up being reminded in an indirect way that "you are worthy because you are a sexual being". I remember as a teenager seeing men check out women, no matter what she was wearing. And I hated men. The only reason I hated men was because of the way they treated women and sexualised women. And people would say to me, "Shouldn't you be angry at women for objectifying themselves?" But I couldn't see that. All I could see was the industry behind it that was still owned by men.'

Culture was inextricably tied up in Waajida's anger at sexism, and added a very personal sheen to the incandescent rage she felt. She viewed it as both an insult and a betrayal; the Arab men she grew up with were unpleasantly sexist and objectifying, and she saw their behaviour as traitorous to the egalitarian and respectful Arab prophet at the centre of the faith she adored.

'I grew up hating Arab men in particular,' she acknowledged. 'And you might say it's Anglo men, it's Greek men, but when I went to the Arab world, I saw it time and time again and that disgusted me. Because the Prophet *salAllahu alayhi wasalam* was an Arab, Muslim man. It's like, "Did you people not learn anything? Did you not learn your *deen*? Is your *deen* just prayer? How can you treat women like that?"'

Ultimately, this anger was not sustainable for Waajida and she spoke of her months of therapy to overcome her fury at the sexism she witnessed growing up. But even though her anger subsided, the situation had not changed. It was through observing the reality around her dispassionately that she felt she could engage with the situation with fresh eyes. 'Women are still objectified,' she said, 'even though I can love men now. Nothing's changed, the reality's still there. Just the hatred is gone. And I felt like now I must work with that, objectively I can say, "That is wrong, how can I change that?"'

Waajida found her reflections distressing, and she again cried as we spoke. But she was clear that she was as deeply committed to her work as she is to Islam, saying 'I operate from a pro-faith perspective because I believe the answer lies within that.' She explained that 'Faith goes right to the deep issue. I'm passionate about women's rights; the other passion I have is Allah. And I realise they cannot be separated. I believe the problems we have in the Muslim world today stem from a lack of understanding of *tawhid, la illaha ilAllah*. Because if we understood that—really understood who Allah is, and who *rasooluLah* [prophet of God], *salAlahu alayhi wasalam* is—we would not have any injustices towards anyone, we would not have sexism, we would not have inequality. I think faith becomes a solution because you're going right to the heart of the problem. And that's what saddens me— because the Muslim world is so far away from the *deen*. If we're still mistreating Indians in Saudi and Dubai, if we're still mistreating women, then we are so far away. We are so distant. Because the first thing the prophet *salAllahu alayhi wasalam* spoke about was equality. The first things that he established were be fair, be equal, be just, have mercy, have compassion.'

Waajida said this is why she works for change from a faith perspective—because it transforms people. Sadly, after working in this area for twenty years, Waajida believed the changes she had seen in the Australian Muslim community regarding sexism were minuscule, with women on mosque boards still a rarity. She said the lack of change saddens her profoundly because it is another betrayal of her faith.

Once again she affirmed her acceptance of the long-term— possibly generational—nature of her work, saying, 'I really was hoping for a better world for my daughter. And to see that she is still struggling to get basic equality from her male Muslim peers? It really is sad and sometimes you do feel like giving up. But then you remember, the Prophet *salAllahu alayhi wasalam* never gave up, he kept going. Our role is not to see results, it's to keep going. It's what you believe in, so you keep going whether you see results or not.'

Given the grim picture Waajida had painted, I asked her why she felt there were not many other women, young or old, doing the work she did? She explained that while there are in fact more

Muslim women than men doing community work—such as mosque tours—women were routinely given the less important roles. 'When it comes to the education, and policy-making and the imams and the mosque committees and the leadership—that is given to men.' She identified the particularly gendered dynamic of the highly respected teaching roles in the Muslim community: 'Women are told constantly, "You don't have the knowledge, who are you?" And then we're limited—women only teach women. Women don't teach men. It's like a no-no. But men can teach women of course, and they can teach men. It's like women humble themselves and go, "Who am I to teach, who am I to give lectures?"'

Beyond access to roles, Waajida also pointed to the lack of support of women in roles such as hers, which can leave women isolated. But even when she feels alone in her work, Waajida still bears an acute sense of responsibility to her community. 'Women just aren't supported, like why would a woman go through all this? So it takes a lot of guts, it takes something inside that you feel, a roar that keeps you going. And maybe not everyone has that. And women are working but they're working silently, they don't come out and say it, like men. Men are like "This is what I do!"'

Waajida's story succinctly illustrates the many threads that form the rope of these women's experiences: the pain, faith, determination and hope. And she was by no means unique in her experiences or feelings.

I wondered, what motivates women like Waajida? What prompts them to turn their attention to the plight of their sisters in faith? I knew from my own experience that fighting sexism in Muslim communities is often a problematic endeavour, so I was curious about whether there had to have been a great impetus to prompt these women to tackle an often-unpopular cause. The stakes would have to be very high for them to risk criticism from Muslim communities to proceed. Indeed, as interviewee Amina Wadud observes in her book *Inside the Gender Jihad*, 'For any who wish to be accepted as truly Muslim, their struggles cannot go beyond established patriarchy or male authorities, otherwise they face the potential consequences of being labelled outsiders to Islam.'

It is worth noting that for many of the women I interviewed, their answer as to why they became involved in the struggle against sexism in Muslim communities was that such a struggle was fundamental to who they are as people. They answered simply with, 'Because I'm a woman' (Karima and Ify), or even 'Because I exist' (Waajida). They also spoke about the motivation for their involvement in the most uncompromising of terms: 'This is vital' (Latifa), 'If you don't speak up, no one is going to give you your rights, you have to fight for them' (Laleh), 'Because there is no place where sexism has ended' (Ayesha), and 'I will die trying' (Daisy). The sheer pathos of these sentiments points to the criticalness and personal nature of the issue for the women, and reveals some of the strength of belief that has sustained them through the challenges they have faced.

When I asked the women to nominate which of the previously mentioned four categories was the most significant reason for them to fight sexism in their communities, the most common was 'a dissatisfaction with the status quo of the alleged "Islamic" perspective or Muslims' attitudes towards women'. Eight of the twenty-three women identified with this first category. The next most significant motivation was their personal history of fighting injustice or trying to fix things. And the last two categories—negative experiences that led to greater questioning, and a desire to see Muslim women be more present, heard and recognised—tied, with nearly a quarter of the twenty-three women citing one or the other as a factor. Four women either do not fit these categories or refused them altogether—one refused to answer; one said she 'just fell into it'; the other two said they did not see themselves as having a specific interest in women's rights, although both have contributed enormously to the field.

Significantly, many of the women identified with more than one motivation for their involvement in fighting sexism. It was not unusual for them to say their dissatisfaction with the status quo along with a desire to see Muslim women in the spotlight as motivators. Indeed, many of the women seemed to float between the categories, depending on the issue or the stage of their respective lives when they addressed it. This suggests that far from being discrete entities, the categories need to be viewed as something fluid. However, I placed the women in the categories with which they most firmly or repeatedly identified as their motivation because, despite the somewhat 'liquid' nature of their reasons, all of them had identified and emphasised a primary motivating force.

It is worth considering why these particular women chose to fight sexism in the first place. That is, many other Muslim women would have viewed the same sexism within their tradition and communities but would not have chosen to respond similarly. Some would have given up and either left their community or Islam all together; others would have internalised the messages and seen the sexist view of women as being divinely mandated; and yet still others would have rejected the situation internally, within themselves, but would have done nothing to change their external circumstance. What was it about these women that prompted them to take the often-costly step of attempting to change things?

A majority of the women I interviewed said it was a frustration or unhappiness with the materials or teachings available to them relating to their faith or their position as women within it that led to them fighting sexism within Muslim communities. And they fought this sexism by filling the gaps they felt had been created by a male-centric understanding and practise of their faith. Associate Professor of Religious Studies Sa'diyya Shaikh, who demonstrates why it is untenable for the patriarchal interpretations of much Islamic theology to be sustained by

Muslim women and why it must be challenged, describes this experience eloquently when she says, 'I am very often left with the uneasy and unpalatable notion that as a female, I am the "Other" within the house of Islam'. She rarely recognises herself in Islamic texts, with the female so often positioned as the other, and reveals that this exclusion is painful. She is determined to demonstrate her rejection of this deeply un-Islamic reality as part of her sincere dedication to her faith: 'This commitment makes it impossible for me to surrender my religion to what I consider to be the *shirk* [associating partners with God, the greatest, and only unforgivable, sin in Islam] of patriarchy.'

The women who fell into this category had different sources that fed their frustration, including the way in which male theologians interpret the Qur'an in relation to women, the absence of successful Muslim women in magazines or online, media representations of Muslim women, the various Muslim communities' lack of public discussion on gender issues, and women's treatment in the *masjid* (mosque). All of these women eventually became involved in creating new knowledge or avenues for a different understanding of Muslim women. As Yvonne Haddad, an academic specialising in Islamic history and Muslim-Christian relations, observes, 'Muslim women in the Muslim world and the diaspora became convinced that it is crucial to participate in creating Islamic knowledge to meet the demands of the 21st century.' I would argue that often the women in this category took the main areas of dissatisfaction listed above and became knowledge producers in order to address this. This is especially true in the case of the theologians, and certainly several of the activists.

For Muslim women, the production of knowledge has been about the power to define themselves. For so long, as many of the women interviewed lamented, everyone else—from Muslim men to non-Muslims, both male and female—have defined Muslim women based on the analysis of Muslim men. In contributing new, female-focussed ways of reading the Qur'an, or offering new ways of understanding how to live as a Muslim woman through magazines and blogs, these women are engaged in knowledge production at the most fundamental level.

Muslim women who are able to operate somewhat outside of male dominance and control are more likely to be knowledge producers. This was exemplified by Amina Wadud, who discussed with me her need to shift away from the expectations of her male supervisors if she was going to be able to produce what became her ground-breaking text, *Qur'an and Woman: Rereading the sacred text from a woman's perspective*. She told me, 'You start to ask questions like, "Where is Islam? What is Islam?" And that was my motivation: to understand directly from Allah through the Qur'an what was the role of women in Islam. [When I started to write about women in Islam] I was discouraged from doing that because it didn't seem scholarly enough to some of my advisors, because scholarly for them was to take the work that was already out there and simply critique it. But I thought, "These men [scholars she was supposed to critique] are not speaking to me."'

She went on to describe how the Qur'anic imperative of being for all people in all times made it untenable for her to accept—wholesale—religious interpretations that were almost entirely male. 'I took it to heart that [the Qur'an] was for everyone … for all times and all places and all people. And without a clear effort by women to understand the Qur'an for themselves and its impact on their lives we are always going to be told part of the story, and maybe not the part that is most beneficial to our faith development.' And thus, for Wadud, this endeavour became a religious mandate. She believed that it was necessary for women to contribute to theological interpretation 'because when Allah gave us the Qur'an for our own guidance, it wasn't just given to men. So it is fundamental to our faith to take the book and seek that guidance and live by that guidance.'

Another woman, Laleh, was similarly driven to engage in female interpretation of the sacred texts after deep disappointment with the written teachings available. She eventually wrote a translation of the entire Qur'an from a woman's perspective. About her translation, she said, 'There are many ways this translation is different from other translations, because I was looking at this from a woman's perspective. There had been one other woman who happens to be Iranian who did do a translation of the Quran, but if you read her translation and you read Yusuf Ali [arguably the most famous English translation of the Qur'an] there is no difference. So it's a problem for a woman to put her name on something and do the same thing that men do when there are issues that need to be addressed. So mine was the first critical English translation of the Qur'an.' For Laleh, this meant focussing on things she felt other, male translators had neglected, such as the gendered nature of the Arabic language. 'I made sure whenever there was a feminine pronoun, that I would indicate that,' she explained.

She went on to tell me why she feels Muslim women fighting sexism was important, 'Because if we don't speak up, no one is going to give us our rights. We have to fight for them. We have to step up to the plate and work for them. Women have a different perspective and our perspective needs to be heard.' Like a number of the other women with whom I'd spoken, Laleh explained this belief using a religious motivation: 'There's a very famous tradition of the Prophet that says "whatever my community has consensus on, cannot be wrong". So for 1400 years they [men] have been saying how there's consensus on this and consensus on that, but they have not taken half the population into account. Where is the woman's voice? That's why Muslim women need to be active so they can challenge things like this.'

Yvonne Haddad makes an important observation about the nature of the work that theologians, like Amina Waddud and Laleh, have produced, and their intention behind it, when she observes, 'Women authors have identified conditions that prompted the patriarchal perspectives that distorted the egalitarian and pluralistic teachings of the divine message of the Qur'an and the Prophetic practice and example. Thus their studies are not presented as an apologetic, a reinterpretation of the heritage of the faith in order to appease the enemies of Islam in the West; rather, their findings are presented as an attempt to recapture the essence of the faith as revealed to the Prophet Muhammad and as practised by their fathers and mothers of the faith under guidance.' That is to say, the women who despaired at the way their faith, and their position as women within it, were presented to them through books and certain events, decided to dig deeper into the resources of their tradition to find the egalitarian and just message they felt sure was inherent. They did so not in order to reassure non-Muslims or to save face in an increasingly hostile globalised world, but out of a strong belief in their faith, and a strong personal need for that message to be apparent to Muslim women.

The next most common category was that of having a strong personal history of fighting injustice. Even when they were children or before they were Muslim, these women were committed to improving situations, especially if they felt inequality was present within them. Zafreen's sentiments were typical of many when she said, 'I've always had a very strong sense of justice and equity. Not just in women's issues, but that's become even stronger. Even in high school, I was part of a small group of girls that fought to have our own girls' common room. And it's just developed more and more because I've seen more and more that Islam is used to really justify a lot of very backward and misogynistic ideas and rules.'

Hakimah, the US army colonel who has been posted to many Muslim-majority countries, told me, 'I'm a do-er, I've always been a do-er, even in elementary school. I'm always the one who looks around and says, "We can do that better, let's work on that, there's a gap here, how do we fill that black hole". I know what it means to be active and passionate and not wait for others to fix the problem when you know you have the skills to help that problem get solved.'

It is unsurprising that personality type or personal history would have a profound influence on these women being willing to fight any sort of injustice they perceive. A number of the women interviewed commented on the significant role their parents played in raising them to be conscious of justice, whether because of the injustice their parents had faced (such as African-Americans in the United States in the 1960s or being displaced Palestinians) or because there was an attitude of service and activism attached to their faith (whether their parents were Muslim or Christian). This is supported by earlier findings by other researchers who found that women's mothers—including mothers being supportive of things like the women's movement and employment after having children—had a positive impact on their daughter adopting feminist attitudes.

The final two categories, comprising equal numbers of women (nearly a quarter each), were the effect of having negative experiences in spurring them to search for 'true Islam'—especially regarding treatment of and attitudes towards women—and a strong desire to ensure that Muslim women were present in the public sphere and had their voices amplified. Several women I interviewed reported situations where they were treated terribly as women in the name of Islam. Surprisingly, these events, far from pushing them away from their religious tradition in horror, propelled them into investigating for themselves what their faith seemed to teach about women, and they were often surprised by what they found. They realised what a one-sided, sexist interpretation of the faith they had encountered. This in turn seemed to lead to a greater, more authentically personal adoption of Islam, something that has been similarly reported by Muslim women in France and Germany.

Nahida told me about the permanent sense of unease she experienced over what she was taught about Islam and women, on the one hand, and what she felt to be true, on the other. And that this created an unbearable tension. 'The male-centric Islamic studies I had been taught since I was very young were constantly at conflict with what I recognised as the truth that provided foundation for my values,' she told me. 'In order to reconcile and find answers I ventured into exegesis and discovered to my amazement that the extracted interpretations that had disturbed me with their sexism were completely un-Islamic and unfounded.'

It has long been known that the determining factor for a woman to support the women's movement or feminist ideals is a personal experience of discrimination or injustice. Adrienne affirmed this finding when I asked her how she became interested in fighting sexism among Muslims. She told me about her abusive ex-husband who used Islam to justify his control of her. 'His perspectives were not out of line with what the tradition has said, he never said anything that could not be supported through the interpretations of scholars. In particular, there was the notion that women please God through pleasing their husbands.' These arguments raised red flags for Adrienne, not just for her personal safety, but for the deeply disconcerting religious implication that ties a man's opinion and divine sanction. As Adrienne put it, 'At a certain point, little by little, no matter how deep into Stockholm Syndrome to a man and the tradition one is, this starts to look like *shirk*.'

Both this and the most common category, dissatisfaction with the status quo, highlight a process identified by Christian feminist theologian Elisabeth Schüssler Fiorenza. First, she says, women experience 'a tension between their own self-understanding and the position of women in society and church', which leads them to 'scrutinize prevailing androcentric theological system'. Then, this 'new insight that theology was formulated by men in the interest of patriarchal male structures' leads women to question the 'prevailing androcentric interpretations of scripture'. Nimat Barazangi describes much the same dissatisfaction when Muslim women become sharply aware that 'they were erroneously made to believe that males' interpretation are as binding as the Qur'anic principles themselves'.

This process can be summarised as the transition from being anxious or unsettled by the status quo to analysing the situation, and then being able to question and even challenge why those things are the way they are. The process Schüssler Fiorenza describes can be put into shorthand, as a movement from tension to scrutinising to questioning. And it is clearly present in the journeys of many of the women I interviewed—both in the negative experiences that lead to greater searching and the dissatisfaction with what is. This suggests that such a process is not unusual in faith-centred women who also struggle with the sexism they find in their traditions and communities. It was this that led to the development of new translations and interpretations of the Qur'an, and new forms of media devoted to discussions of gender, Islam and Muslim women.

What is significant for the women I interviewed is that each added something crucial to Schüssler Fiorenza's formulation: knowledge production. In this they created new, anti-sexist ways of being authentically Muslim women, or uncovering old egalitarian ways that had been obscured. And they were not just enacting it for themselves, but spreading the knowledge to other Muslim women (and men) through books, classes, speeches, programs, protests and online posts. This final step was where my participants did something concrete with their experiences and filled an existing hole in Muslim communities: spread their knowledge through various media. And this creation was the solidified culmination of their challenging sexism among Muslims. I saw this process in many of the women I talked to. They moved through the stages of tension to scrutinising to questioning, but then also extending their experience with knowledge production.

Ify's negative experience illustrates this process well. What she faced as a woman trying to pray in the mosque and the ensuing tension she felt led her to investigate orthodox Islamic traditions on the matter of where women should pray in mosques. This then eventually led to her joining with other like-minded women to protest their experiences in mosques.

Asma Uddin also discussed how this process of moving through the stages of tension to scrutinising to questioning and finally to knowledge production played out in her own faith journey as a woman, and how it led her to want to change things. She spoke to me clearly and passionately about her experience of tension when it came to gender and Islam: 'Until the end of high school I had a simple, warm attitude towards Islam, thinking it was completely in line with everything that I thought was good. But once I started college, these simplistic notions got really complicated. I saw very strict notions on campus [from other Muslims] about how women should dress and behave and their place in life. This was really startling, especially because around this time I also started wearing the headscarf. I felt like I was seeing a lot of instances where it was being used precisely as a tool of oppression. And this really complicated my relationship with it and other gender issues in Islam.'

This tension then led to her scrutinising and questioning, just as it had for a number of my other participants. Asma added, 'So I started doing a lot of personal research, online and in books. I started reading Imam al Ghazali, a scholar I loved, and I reached his chapter on women and it was all about how women are there to facilitate men's spirituality. And so there was all this stuff I was reading on the internet, and all this stuff I was experiencing in my personal life, and then there were these classical sources, it was shocking. And then three years into college 9/11 happened. So there was this building crescendo, and then that happened.'

Asma Uddin's experience created something of a perfect storm of cognitive dissonance over what she felt to be true about Islam, and what she was encountering. This prompted her to delve more deeply into her faith: 'And it was around then that I started to understand more about different interpretations, and I separated out that these are just one interpretation [of how women are viewed in Islamic thought] and based on male-centred, male-driven scholarship. It was also the point I put aside analytical stuff, and started to think more, be more philosophical. And I realised there just couldn't be gender inequality. We couldn't have been created like that ... And I realised I wasn't the only one to go through this.'

This realisation of the commonality of her experience propelled Asma to create a space—first in person and then online—of knowledge sharing and production with other Muslim women who were similarly struggling with issues around gender. She said, 'I started a book club and discussion group where we got together to discuss gender issues, and we read books on this issue, and we had guest speakers. And there was so much catharsis, people were crying and sharing their stories, and they were so grateful for it and saying, "We've never had a forum like this before." And that's what sort of triggered it—tonnes of women are going through this, there's a need for a forum and there's no forum. All these women are intelligent, thoughtful, but you don't want it to be academic, because that can be inaccessible. But it can't just be a blog where people say anything or rant. So that was the idea, and [AltMuslimah] was developed. Now I feel like I went through all this for a reason.'

It is significant that it was negative experiences surrounding what it meant to be a Muslim woman that ultimately led to these women re-committing to their faith and working towards fighting sexism among Muslims. For other women, this no doubt would have been the point when they quietly departed from their faith heritage. But for the women with whom I spoke, their frustrating and at times painful experiences were the forges that purified and strengthened their attachment to Islam.

Changing the way Muslim women are perceived by and presented to Muslim and non-Muslim communities was an issue a number of women addressed in their motivation. Several felt especially compelled because they were convinced that the idea of the oppressed, silent Muslim woman who always has a man speak on her behalf was such a dishonour to the tradition of strong Muslim women. Others were annoyed and upset by men always being up the front, as Waajida articulated when she said, 'I have an interest in working with Muslim women, because women have always been, unfortunately, misrepresented, mistreated in the Muslim community and the wider community. Not just in the Muslim community but in the wider community too, women have always been misrepresented, men have always spoken on our behalf, we've never had a voice in history and in the present. We have to speak for ourselves, and all of the programs I've helped to create are to give women a voice to speak for themselves.'

Tayyibah also highlighted the way her work as a magazine editor was, in part, motivated by the desire to counteract the caricatured mainstream portrayal of Muslim women. Her experience was informed by the additional layer of upbringing and being forced to endure racist stereotyping and the widespread absence of black faces and voice in mainstream culture: 'Growing up in the 1960s in the United States, no people of colour were shown positively in the media. Even though both my parents were professionals, as were the adults in my extended family, there was still a sense that there was something wrong with us as a people, a sense of inferiority, a sense of something being amiss. And I remember very distinctly picking up my first copy of *Ebony* magazine and having an epiphany—a sense of self-validation and a sense of power. And I see that experience mirrored every time a Muslim woman picks up *Azizah* magazine for the first time—there's this validation of self.'

She also added, 'We're bombarded with all of these negative images of us which are so different to who we truly are. So that was probably the genesis, the seed, somewhere in the back of my mind or soul, because I grew up in that situation where people of colour were depicted so horribly or not at all. And that's the same with Muslim women—we're depicted as terrorists or victims or the mindless non-entity, or not at all.'

It was these experiences and this awareness that made Tayyibah feel compelled to share the positive stories about Muslim women she knew were out there. She told me, 'Being motivated to give voice to so many of the fabulous stories that we have and the women that have done so many remarkable things was definitely a motivation. And I think it helps establish something of an equilibrium in terms of images and stories of Muslim women. For centuries we've either been defined by Muslim men, or by people who aren't Muslim. So I see *Azizah* magazine as an opportunity for Muslim women to define themselves and set their own agenda.'

Such motivations appear to be firmly rooted in the idea of self-actualisation through honouring their religious histories— this emerged repeatedly as a kind of overarching theme. A strong commitment to their religion was prominent among the women I interviewed; the vast majority identified themselves as pursuing women's rights and opposing injustice and inequality as an expression of their faith. It is not simply that they believed their faith was at least useful in the fight against sexism and could then function as a strong driver in their work within Muslim communities; rather, they came across as whole-heartedly convinced that the sexism they witnessed within their own communities represented an insult to, and gross perversion of, their faith, and that they felt compelled to correct it. The women also seemed convinced that their desire to address misogyny was not some innovation or an external practice, but something deeply embedded within the faith and divinely ordained.

As Nahida told me: 'I am definitely of the perspective that religion is the key to liberating women—that feminist purpose was its very objective in revelation.' She went on to say, 'Religion does not belong to men. It simply needs to be reclaimed by women to be employed for the very cause that it was introduced: to free the oppressed and bring peacefulness and goodness. One of the most important tools is useable resources—aspects of the religion, texts or practices that when rightfully seized by women once more enable women to reacquire the rights that were given to them by God from the very beginning.'

Nahida seems to be providing empirical evidence to support the idea that religiously nourished illnesses require religious solutions (Maguire, 2007)—that the only effective way to address this malaise is through resources provided by the faith itself. Waajida also spoke powerfully about the spiritual imperative in her fight against sexism when she said, 'I'm after equality the way Allah intended us to be. I'm after living with the opposite gender the way Allah intended us to live. If we constantly have inequality—sexism, racism—you do not have the opportunity for spiritual growth, as you're constantly hovering around these barriers. It's like keeping the poor man busy with trying to find food for the next meal, so they're too busy to think about overtaking the government. That's the reason we want equality, it's a higher purpose. Not just because I want equality, but because Allah intended it that way! It's my God-given right, how dare you take it away from me.'

None of the women told me they saw Islam as inherently problematic in the fight for women's rights. In fact, any abuse of women's rights and autonomy was generally identified as a violation of Islamic principles or teachings, and not a consequence of it. They are by no means suggesting their communities are feminist utopias—far from it. Instead, they recognise the conditions under which they must operate while still championing what they perceive to be the egalitarian and just teachings of their faith.

Significantly, several women fell into more than one category, resulting in them straddling two (or more) of them. This demonstrates what a multifaceted and complex issue it was for the women, and how, by falling into more than one category, their motivation to change things was often intensified. Tayyibah, for instance, was motivated both by her desire to amplify Muslim women's voices—'to give voice to so many of the fabulous stories that we have and the women that have done so many remarkable things was definitely a motivation'—and by the experience of living in Saudi Arabia, which made her realise that what she had been taught about Islam's attitudes towards women may not have been the full story. This then led to greater questioning: 'I spent nearly seven years in Saudi Arabia. While I was there I was fortunate enough to study in several different places, and one was a Qur'an school where we had very learned women from many places. And one of the things I took away from my time in Saudi Arabia was that you can be equally pious and equally striving to please Allah, and come up with very different conclusions. More important than the conclusion you come up with is the *daleel*, or reasoning or logic, that you use to get to that point. That really spoke to me, that so often we take things without really delving into the true meaning. And I came back from Saudi Arabia with a firm understanding of being able to acknowledge and appreciate differences that we may have as Muslims and not expect uniformity. And being very adamant that women are equal partners.'

Other women also refused to be reduced to any single category. Asma Uddin, for example, discussed how it was a combination of a negative experience prompting further investigation of the orthodox Islamic view of women, coupled with dissatisfaction with the lack of groups or websites on gender that led her to create the AltMuslimah. Ify reflected on how unpleasant incidents at some mosques, as well as a general dissatisfaction with women's spaces at many mosques, led her to question what the original teachings were for women's inclusion in the mosque, and prompted her activism. And Waajida talked about her desire to see Muslim women up front and represented, coupled with disappointment with the current services and organisations on offer that led her to pioneer Amani Services. That the women didn't statically remain in a single category, but often transcended more than one, or sometimes drifted between them, demonstrates the multifaceted nature of Muslim women's experiences fighting sexism and the layers to their motivations.

The works and lives of these women are all about resisting dominant sexist practices and attitudes within Muslim communities. These women are actively resisting sexism and their responses demonstrate an active reconfiguring not only of power in Muslim communities, but also of the landscape in which power operated in Muslim communities. Interestingly, it is their commitment to Islam that is their greatest inspiration for resisting inequality. But how do other Muslims respond to the endeavours of these women?

Four

ENCOURAGEMENT, HOSTILITY, APATHY

> The words 'feminism' and 'gender equality' and 'sexism' are imbued with some heavy assumptions, and so this work often gets mixed reviews. Some Muslims feel so under siege in predominantly non-Muslim countries that they think we're contributing to 'airing our dirty laundry' or making the community look bad. Other Muslims see a real need for our work, and so are supportive.
>
> — *Ghayda*

While the motivations and journeys of my participants are important, the responses they receive from other Muslims are equally significant. The way other Muslims react to the work being done by women like those I interviewed can motivate and inspire, or they can discourage, hinder and silence. When the response is particularly hostile, it can provoke intense soul-searching and self-doubt.

It is not unusual for women in any community who identify as feminist or engage in activities that could be deemed as feminist to receive criticism or a lack of support from various quarters. And religious communities can often direct specifically gendered attacks against women who challenge the status quo. One woman I spoke to, Amina Wadud, was called a 'she-devil' and a 'whore' by her detractors at a protest against her female-led prayer, saying she had taken herself outside of Islam in her belief that it was theologically permissible for a woman to lead men in ritual prayer. This mimics the accusations levelled at Christian and Jewish women who also attempted to enter the traditionally male fields of power and influence. Women were often punished for challenging the present circumstances, through sexual teasing or harassment and by being labelled as 'sluts' or 'man-chasing'. Such practices have a long history in religious institutions, where female speakers or prophetesses were accused of being seductresses or even prostitutes, despite many of the women accused being celibate. Such tactics are frequently used against women who dare to challenge or speak out in Muslim (or any religious) communities and they often have the desired result of silencing them. It is therefore unsurprising that Muslim women I spoke with would experience similarly negative reactions.

Despite the sometimes incredibly disapproving and even hostile responses the women reported, the vast majority felt they received more support than criticism from other Muslims. This was a surprise to me, as I started this project expecting most of them to say they received a higher degree of criticism and censure. At the same time, a significant proportion of the women I chatted with believed the various Muslim communities did not view fighting sexism as important, showing that the women still felt they had an uphill battle.

Azizah magazine was the first magazine for Muslim women in the United States. Its founding editor, Tayyibah, had told how she suffered as a black child because of the absence of representations in the US mainstream media with which she could identify. This was what shaped and fuelled her desire for Muslim women and girls not to have the same experience. She spoke to me about the profound effect that picking up *Azizah* has had on Muslim women, but she also shared the hostility she has experienced from some Muslims.

'When the first issue came out,' she said, 'I had calls from men telling me "it was *haram*, you're going to hell, you cannot have a magazine cover with women on it." And I had some women calling and writing saying, "This is not good, women shouldn't be on a cover of a magazine, you're imitating Westerners." I got one phone call that said, "What if a non-Muslim man gets this magazine and tears out the picture of Muslim women and puts it up on his wall?" I was flippant and said, "You think we're going to be competing with *Playboy*?"'

She explained to me that, at the time, Muslim women being 'visible and audible' made many people uncomfortable, 'especially those who had defined a pious Muslim woman as a quiet one'. The objections changed over time. 'It started with, "Don't have a woman on the front—have a bowl of fruit or a picture of flowers or a nice meal". And I said if it were a magazine about food, I would, but this is a magazine about Muslim women.' She insisted that she believed strongly 'that a woman's modesty of speech and dress is her passport to public space … My whole thing is that your modesty gives you permission to be in mixed company or the public space. So I think just having a woman on the cover and having her stories prominent has been a big step in asserting equality.' The objections morphed further, 'to "Don't have a pretty woman on the cover" or "She shouldn't smile", or "She shouldn't wear make-up", or "She should look down".' Tayyibah said she was at least relieved when the criticisms 'left the cover and moved on to the content of the magazine, which I could appreciate because it was about substance'.

I asked Tayyibah if she felt she had received more encouragement than discouragement for what she does. She answered without hesitating: 'Definitely, definitely more encouragement. I would say 90 to 95 per cent of the first responses were positive, and it's remained so. They were especially pleased with the quality of the magazine; it can be on the shelf with any other mag.

It was uplifting for [Muslim consumers] to have something that was high quality.'

Unsurprisingly, the women I interviewed felt that other women were the group of people who most supported their work. Nearly half of my participants named other women—whether female friends, family members or strangers—as their greatest champions. The next most often-cited group was Muslim men and/or male Muslim leaders. Very few of my participants claimed non-Muslims offered them the most support.

It seems logical that other women would be the ones to relate to the negative experiences that prompted these women to engage in their work and appreciate their desire for change. And, indeed, the evidence from my interviews supports this, with many of the women saying they received support from other women who could relate to what they were doing and why. Ify stated that women contacted her to show their support, saying, '"Thank you for saying what we've always felt," but they couldn't say it for fear of being branded a feminist or a trouble-maker.' Asra told me that the women who supported her said they did so because they too 'had experienced humiliation at the mosque'. And Ayesha reported that women supported her work said to her, 'Finally, we're talking about these things that have been going on for ages but no one is talking about.' Umaymah similarly highlighted the sense of relief that often accompanied displays of support, primarily from women, 'who are just grateful that there are people who will speak up against the machine of misogyny'. It is thus this sense of identification with shared experiences and assent to common—if not always articulated—convictions that inclined other women to support their work.

Of the women who said other women supported them, it was typical for them to name younger women as their main support base. Zafreen said teenage girls tell her that her work strikes 'a chord and really validated their experiences', and that a film she made told one of their stories. Amina echoed this, telling me that while her book '*Qur'an and Woman* is twenty years old,' to this day young girls approach her and say 'your book changed my life'. She says, 'I feel very blessed to have people respond to me that way. It's 90 per cent women that do, and 10 per cent men, who are usually scholars who acknowledge the benefit of the work. But women acknowledge it for the benefit in their lives.'

Why only 90 per cent? Research outside of Muslim communities has shown that there will always be women who are adamantly opposed to endeavours or ideas that are seen to be feminist. One of the main reasons for non-Muslim women's resistance to the (non-Muslim) feminist movement in the United States and Canada is because they believed it devalued the institutions of church and family, and especially that it was corrosive to the prestige and status of the female home-maker. There was and continues to be a similar sentiment in Muslim attitudes towards feminism—although these attitudes are further complicated and intensified by such historical factors as the experience of colonialism and the secularist presumptions in and of capitalism. It is thus unsurprising that some Muslim women feel a certain sense of unease about the goals of, and indeed the motivations behind, the work of my participants.

Ify framed this particularly well. She told me that Muslims are strongly averse to Western feminism because they think it's destroying the family, 'So when they hear about it, they think it's Western and imposed.' And yet other Muslims, especially women, are frustrated by the contradiction at work in this resistance: 'We're told to excel in our education but we're not allowed to challenge anything at the mosque,' Ify said, sighing.

Notwithstanding this, more than a third of my participants named 'Muslim men' as their second most supportive group. These men included young men, old men, imams and community leaders, family members and their husbands. Often, the women who named Muslim men as their strongest supporters also named Muslim men among their fiercest detractors. This is in no way surprising when we remember that Muslim communities are not a homogenous mass, feeling the same way about all issues. Islamic Studies scholar Mona Hassan's research into Turkish women preachers supported these findings: the women in her study also named their male colleagues as some of their greatest supporters, while at the same time, other imams and the husbands of some of the women who wanted to attend their lessons as their strongest critics. Just as there are some men in the non-Muslim community who support feminism and others who despise it, so too Muslim men.

It was not unusual for my participants to name an imam who had been particularly supportive and, in the same breath, name other imams or leaders who had made their lives very difficult. Waajida demonstrated this well when I asked her about people who had supported her. She said that she was 'pleasantly surprised' at the support that she found among male Muslim leaders in Egypt. 'The *shaykh* [learned religious leader], my teacher, who I used to go and recite Qur'an to, he was amazing. He had no problem sitting in front of women, women reciting Qur'an to him with *tajwid* [melodious, traditional way of reciting Qur'an].' And yet, she lamented, such a thing would be 'unheard of' in Australia. In fact, she admitted, that one of the most steadfast sources of discouragement was her own religious teacher in Australia. 'He discouraged me in a roundabout way. The sarcasm. If I offered my opinion in a meeting, he would say, "Why don't you discuss that with your husband on the way home first, then raise it with us" … Or he would tell me to organise a program and I would organise it and present it to him—and it would have taken a lot of work to put together—and he'd just bypass it and just do what he wanted to do. So after a while you realise you're not going to be as good as the men. And I never wanted to make it a gender thing, but it is a gender thing.'

Some of the other women, such as Ayesha Mattu, specifically singled out their husbands as a source of support so vital they would not be able to do their work without them. She told me, 'If not for a husband who follows the *sunnah* [the way of the Prophet Muhammad] of helping at home with the baby and giving me creative space' her book, *Love, InshaAllah*, simply would not exist. Ingrid similarly told me that her husband is 'extremely supportive', and that her work would have been impossible 'without his support and encouragement'. Likewise, Adrienne told me that her partner 'will make space for me and do whatever he can for me to carry on with my gender-justice work'.

Contrary to the pervasive stereotype of Muslim men being aggressively misogynistic and Muslim marriages the bastion of female oppression, it is clear that, in the experiences of at least some of my participants, the support from their husbands is not only welcome but also crucial to their success.

Just as these women found support and encouragement from a variety of sources, discouragement and outright hostility also came from different quarters and in varying degrees. Some said they were confronted by very little discouragement; others felt they were criticised from many directions. The group most often named as sources of discouragement were Muslim men, including imams, leaders, teachers, mosque committee members and the 'average Muslim man on the street', with one in three participants naming this category of people.

Some of this discouragement comes in the form of an almost visceral reaction on the part of the men to a perceived threat posed by women. I asked Malika, for instance, why she thought so many Muslim men have such a strong reaction to words like feminism or sexism. She said a term like feminism 'gives women strength, and it might put men on their toes'. She used the example of attempts to identify and address forms of domestic violence within Muslim communities. Malika told me that she has had to 'soften it down' to such an extent that she now speaks in terms of 'merciful partnerships'. She told me, 'when I first started out and used the term "domestic violence", imams felt from the outset we were putting an accusation against men.' Likewise, 'using sexism or feminism put them on the defensive and felt they were being blamed. And it put them as being victims because they said we were judging them without talking with them. And I've found I really have to soften it down just to get them to be part of the dialogue.'

Malika provided a striking example of using 'nego-feminism' to achieve her goal. Nego-feminism is a term coined by Obioma Nnaemeka of Indiana University to describe the feminism she saw occurring in Africa: 'First, nego-feminism is the feminism of ne-gotiation; second, nego-feminism stands for "no ego feminism".' Nnaemeka states that many African cultures share values founded on 'the principles of negotiation, give and take, compromise, and balance'. That negotiation comprises a 'double meaning of "give and take/exchange" and "cope with successfully/go around".' Therefore feminism, as she has seen practised in Africa, 'challenges through negotiations and compromise'. She says, it 'knows when, where, and how to detonate patriarchal land mines; it also knows when, where, and how to go around patriarchal land mines. In other words, it knows when, where, and how to negotiate with or negotiate around patriarchy in different contexts.'

Malika recognised how she needed to carefully negotiate the agitation that Muslim men felt about her domestic violence project, altering her approach accordingly. While such an approach may seem too soft or too accommodating of things that do not warrant such consideration, at its heart nego-feminism is deeply pragmatic. Those who employ it recognise that a gentler, more embracing approach can still achieve the same goal without being too combative. This can be quite different to the standard Western feminist approach. As Nnaemeka explains, 'The language of feminist engagement in Africa (collaborate, negotiate, compromise) runs counter to the language of Western feminist scholarship and engagement (challenge, disrupt, deconstruct, blow apart, etc.).'

It would be wrong, however, to say that nego-feminism is the natural fit for all Muslims. Other women I interviewed employed techniques that take on a more disruptive, challenging approach, such as the previously mentioned pray-ins run by Ify that had them evicted from the mosque by the local police at the insistence of the male mosque committee.

The second largest group nominated by my participants—named by nearly a quarter of the women—was not so much a category of people but a group of people united by an attitude. Specifically, it was a diverse range of Muslims united solely by their disapproval of these women for 'shaming the community' or 'airing the community's dirty laundry' by openly challenging sexism. So Adrienne, who was subjected to domestic violence in her first marriage, said that, when she first 'came out' about her abuse, some Muslim women wrote her emails encouraging her to 'hide her "shame"'. Likewise, after a particular article that she had written, Asra told me that she received emails telling her to apologise for 'shaming the community'. Her parents also found themselves ostracised from circles of long-standing friends.

That shaming a community or communities is viewed with such gravity reflects the common sense among many Muslims in the West that they are under attack. It is such that any act appearing to give more fodder to this hostile audience is seen as tantamount to treason. This phenomenon in Western Muslim communities can be especially pernicious and debilitating, as commentator (and my husband) Waleed Aly argues in his book:

> This same defensiveness also underlies the common anxiety in Western Muslim communities to present a unified front. It is as though the situation is one of rival tribes, where unity is a show of strength, and any hint of division is death. What is less often understood is just how dangerous this fake veneer of unity is in the present environment. We live in an age where, fairly or unfairly, the dominant images surrounding

Islam and Muslim populations are manifestly ugly. A rigid determination to appear united (which usually ends up meaning homogenous) does little more than unify masses of Muslims with that ugliness … That many Muslims are so desperate to fit within this unhealthy category for the sake of some phoney 'strength', particularly when the reality is exactly the opposite, is evidence of a thoroughly defensive posture.

It is thus seen as far better for Muslim women to keep quiet about the sexism that occurs within Muslim communities than to risk inviting more condemnation from a wider community whose prejudices have been vindicated.

The third largest group—identified by one in five of my participants—was again a knot of diverse people united not by demography but attitude. These were the Muslims who criticised my participants as 'Muslim women behaving badly'; that is, for behaving in a manner that was deemed un-Islamic. Some of this criticism was stated in an indirect way. Two women reported that they knew of strong criticism against them, but only heard about it through secondary sources and gossip. So Karima reported that she will 'only hear second and third hand that I'm considered a radical feminist and people should keep their daughters away from me'. When discussing the criticism that she received for her book, Ayesha told me, 'We heard third-person that people were saying it's un-Islamic and that we're normalising the *haram*, but no one has said that to us.'

At other times the criticism was overt. Jessica told me how common it is to be told that 'we're not very good Muslims' in comments on their website. One such comment informed them, 'You're trying to change Islam and you don't even pray.' Jessica noted how 'bizarre' this was given the comment was from someone who didn't know any of her website staff personally. She said the comments are particularly 'nasty and really offensive' whenever they post articles on LGBTI issues. 'It can be disheartening that we're working really hard and then certain people respond and you feel you are never good enough.' Ify reported similar experiences: 'They say, "You're causing *fitna*, you're a troublemaker". They called us "rebellious women" for praying behind men at the *masjid*.'

All of this criticism can be seen as many attempts to control or silence the women into behaving in ways deemed more appropriate or acceptable by Muslim communities. Such control can be quite subtle, in that there is no explicit request or order for the women to stop doing their work. Instead, action is taken to call into question the religious legitimacy of what they are doing. For example, Laleh reports a man criticising her in a newspaper interview for not studying Arabic long enough to be able to do a proper translation of the Qur'an, despite her years of tertiary study in the field. A public display of a lack of support is a similar tactic, as happened to Ayesha with her controversial book. She told me about a large Muslim book club of up to a hundred members which had selected her book for study, then publicly de-selected it, informing all their members that Ayesha's book was, in fact, *haram*. 'And apparently they had a list of people on Facebook saying, "Ditto. We agree that this is *haram*".' Ayesha informed me wryly. 'So that's been an interesting thought police, because apparently this group of women sets the tone for what is acceptable or not in their community.' Actions like these are indeed tools used to silence, even if not explicitly stated as such.

Two of the women I interviewed were condemned because they either didn't wear hijab or their hijab was deemed inadequate. When I asked Karima about any discouragement she received in her efforts to eradicate sexism among Muslims, she told me, 'There are converts who jump into Islam boots and all and immediately start wearing hijab, and there are those like me who take their time and think about it and either accept or reject different aspects of Islamic culture. And I chose to reject all the dress part of it, and this upset a lot of people in the community who really sincerely believe that you must wear hijab and must always wear a long dress. So not many people said anything but certainly a few did. One gentleman in particular, every time he saw me, would comment and give me a lecture on why I must wear hijab, and when I just wore a scarf loosely around my head, he would comment loudly, "Oh, there's sister Karima, wearing half a hijab".' Zafreen responded similarly, saying, 'There is a minority who don't feel I have the authority to talk about issues affecting Muslims and especially affecting Muslim women because I don't wear the veil.'

It is important to note the significance such censure has, even if done behind the women's backs. Criticising the religious legitimacy, modesty of dress or general propriety of either the actions or very personhood of these women can be a very powerful technique used to control and censor. This is linked in no small way to the importance reputation has for Muslim women, as sociologist Sana al-Khayyat says, Muslim women are 'very conscious of … any accusation of acting dishonourably'. As Waajida powerfully put it, 'Our reputations are everything. So we're stuck. Do we serve the community, do we do what we think is right, do we provide an alternative, and take that risk of being branded a feminist and this and that?'

Targeting the reputation of Muslim activist women in order to exert control over them is not just confined to the Australian and North American Muslim communities. As Colette Harris found in her research of Muslim women in Tajikistan, 'the word 'ayb [immodesty, shame] can be wielded like a sword to keep order'. And as is patently obvious from many of these examples, such criticism is intentionally gendered.

I asked the women if they thought their reception in Muslim communities was due, at least in part, to their gender. In other words, did they believe that the response they received would be different, more positive, if they were saying the same things about sexism among Muslims or undertaking the same actions (writing about it, having pray-ins in the mosque, developing programs against domestic violence) but were men? Amina's response was categorical: 'I think if I were a man saying anything I would be received more positively.' Jessica responded similarly, saying, 'Yes. I think that the people who police our Muslim-ness would probably treat us differently if we were men.' Karima agreed: 'I used to practice as an accountant and the brothers at one of the mosques in Sydney had a tax claim issue. And I fixed it for them. And after I fixed it, they got up in the masjid and thanked my husband for fixing it, even though he had nothing to do with it. And they thanked him because they couldn't thank me. And it's the way they are—women are put down and ignored.'

Other women reported similar experiences, and they all demonstrate the complicated relationship that Muslim communities have with sexism, patriarchal beliefs and practices, and who has the legitimacy to challenge them. One of the more troubling aspects that struck me while I was thinking through the reflections from my various interviews, was the fact that the group of women who struggled most to nominate supporters among Muslims were the older Australian women who were the pioneers of the fight against sexism within their communities. When I first noticed this trend I wondered if it was mirrored in the experiences of the older North American women—perhaps it was a product of the time in which their activism took place. But it was not.

Of the four older North American Muslim women I interviewed, two were African-American converts, one was an Iraqi convert, and one was South Asian who was born and raised as a Muslim. Cultural anthropologist Carolyn Rouse has examined the different ways in which Muslims gain membership to the group or *ummah*, and argues that for many it is based on nationalities or races that are traditionally tied to Muslim heritage. She goes on to say, 'This is clearly not the case for African-American converts who must prove they are Muslims through their knowledge and practice of their faith.' This process of 'proving' can be difficult in the face of sceptical Muslim communities, who may have negative, pre-conceived ideas that African-American Muslims are really from the Nation of Islam,[1] viewed by most Sunni Muslims to be heretics and outside the fold of authentic Islam. Simply being black and a convert was enough to warrant suspicion for some of the pioneering women I interviewed, such as Amina Wadud. When I asked Amina if being a convert affected the way other Muslims treated her and her work, she said that it had 'affected the way [my] legitimacy has been challenged and opportunities that may have been available to brown men are not open to me. I wish it were better but I don't think I'll live long enough to see it get better, so I just keep trying.'

It is therefore easier for other Muslims to dismiss African-American convert women who challenge sexism in ways they might find uncomfortable by considering their 'knowledge and practice of faith' to be lacking, as Rouse describes. That women like Amina don't always wear hijab and do divisive things—like lead men and women in mixed-gender prayer—means that their group membership can be challenged by other, 'real' Muslims. Laleh's experience of dismissive suspicion from other Muslims further illustrates that automatic membership into the group simply because of ethnicity is also debatable. She spoke about how people viewed her as controversial because she was Iraqi, and thus Sunni Muslims (who form the vast majority of the global Muslim population) assumed she was Shia (the religious majority in Iraq, and the smaller of Islam's two major sects). However, the other two pioneering American women (one African-American convert, the other of South Asian background) did not raise similar issues relating to background and group membership, despite working in areas that are similarly challenging to community norms.

Of these four groundbreaking North American Muslim women, three were divorced and one was still married to a man she considered very supportive of women's rights. Only one wore the hijab permanently. They were all grandmothers, and were forerunners in their activism and theology, yet all of them said they had received much more support than discouragement, and they all seemed very upbeat and connected to a community in their own way. Even when recounting negative stories, they often laughed and joked about what had happened to them—such as Laleh being laughingly dismissive about an influential male leader's criticism of the standard of her Arabic, and Tayyibah's amusement at the suggestion that having women in hijab on her magazine's cover could somehow compete with *Playboy*. The humour of these women pointed to an underlying resilience that allowed them to continue, even in the face of personal and professional adversity.

It is difficult to know exactly why it was that the Australian women reported so much less support and seemed much more despondent about their experiences. But I suspect it was, at least in part, a function of the different natures of the North American and Australian Muslim communities. The Australian Muslim community as an established group is much smaller and younger than its American counterpart, and it thus offers less opportunity for support and for finding like-minded people. Its demography and history are also different. I wondered if the fact that American Muslims had had to grapple with a civil rights movement based entirely on alleviating discrimination helped to create an attitude that was more adept at confronting prejudice than what the Australian women experienced. Indeed, a distinctly 'American' attitude came through in many of the conversations I had with American women that was not there with the Australian women with whom I spoke—attitudes that seemed to be predicated on the obligation to serve their communities and country, a strong self-belief and the feeling that if there was a problem to be fixed, they should take personal responsibility for fixing it. These sentiments were mostly absent among the Australian women I interviewed, who seemed more uncertain of themselves, more in a position of leadership and change either unwillingly or due to circumstance as opposed to personal ambition, and more personally affected by criticisms by their local Muslim community.

Listening to the three oldest Australian women recount their stories was incredibly sad for me. These were the most pained and painful stories I heard. They had all experienced real loneliness and isolation in their work, and the sting of their negative experiences still lingered. Two were converts and one was born a Muslim of Middle Eastern background who immigrated to Australia when she was young, and it seemed that the years they spent chipping away in an area with little support and a lot of criticism had left these women, at times, dejected. Not in God or their faith, but at a community that hadn't supported them when they needed it most.

Latifa's story illustrated their experience well. She confessed that encouragement from Muslims was 'hard to find' and that her first attempt at fairly modest activism 'had no support from local Muslim community'. Not only would they not 'attend openings or functions', she told me, 'but they took advantage of the childcare centre without giving anything back'. Muslims would 'see what I'm doing as challenging the status quo and get nervous and suspicious and try to contain what I'm doing. I've certainly had my battles. I started the first Islamic childcare and after-school care centre in Adelaide but I was eventually totally disenfranchised from that so it could be put into the hands of a different group. Not just discouraged—I was threatened. They said if I didn't withdraw my name from the centre, my name would be blackened overseas, that I'd never be able to raise money overseas. So there's been a fair bit of pressure on me not to continue my work. When I was running the after-school care centre during the school holidays, I'd say one thing at assembly, the kids would go to *jummah* [congregational prayers held at the mosque every Friday] and a male would stand up and totally undercut what I'd previously said. And I could do very little about it, because I didn't have the Islamic scholarship to challenge and silence them, and I didn't have enough men who saw things the same way I did.'

I asked Latifa who had been an inspiration to her, or a mentor. There was a long silence. Finally, she responded, 'To be honest, not many in the Muslim community. There were no females ahead of me. When I set out there was nobody who was prominent. I had women I worked with, but I've been at the head of the game so there have not been many people. And it makes it much, much harder as you're constantly questioning yourself and there's very few people who can give you guidance. I haven't had that.' She did acknowledge that when she went through a period of particular difficulty, she found inspiration in the labours of Saint Mary Mackillop, the Australian nun. 'I'd never been Catholic. But she's regarded so highly yet she was excommunicated and she had to battle the bishops.'

That two of the three pioneering Australian Muslim women I interviewed were converts may go some way—though not the whole way—towards explaining their experiences as they lacked the support of a cultural community within the existing Muslim communities that other Muslim women may have had. The third woman, who was a born Muslim of Arab background, broke down in tears when I asked her about any encouragement she received, saying how she had never received support, even from the organisation within which she worked as a young woman. Thus, there is more at play here than merely the act of being a convert. However, I believe it did play a significant role for the two Anglo convert women I interviewed, as not only were they torchbearers in terms of fighting sexism, but they were also trailblazers in terms of being public, well-known convert women, which itself would have led to terrible isolation in communities that were very small and deeply fragmented along ethnic lines.

Without the support of a specific cultural group behind them, these two women were very much on their own—as Latifa attests,

'The local community, because it's ethnically based and I'm not ethnic and don't affiliate with an ethnic group, have been really reluctant to support me. It's a matter of "Who do you think you are?"' This was exacerbated by the fact that Latifa was married to a convert man from Russia, and Karima's husband, though born Muslim, died and left Karima widowed relatively early. I asked Karima if she felt being a convert played a role in the difficulties or isolation she experienced? 'Yes,' she answered, 'people don't come out and say things, but certainly people like me and other converts like Latifa, we always get the impression we're never accepted as part of the community.'

All of my participants have borne a heavy toll for their efforts to fight sexism among Muslims. So I was keen to ask them how they felt Muslim and non-Muslim communities regarded their struggle—was it worthwhile, necessary, or something less positive? Of the women who answered the question, more than a third felt Muslims didn't view fighting sexism as positive at all. Their responses were as mild as, 'It's not a priority' (Umaymah and Malika), and as despairing as, 'We're not even having the dialogue. It's way too threatening for men to hear it' (Waajida). More than half of them said that there are profound differences among Muslims on the issue; that some Muslims saw it as important and some didn't. Only one woman said Muslims as a whole saw it as important.

Those who believed that the struggle against sexism among Muslims was viewed entirely negatively by Muslims gave a number of reasons for this. For some, like Umaymah, the struggle was always going to be viewed as incongruous with Muslim belief: 'No matter how far we've traversed, the community instantly looks at that as "feminism". And it's minimised down to, "You can't be feminist and Muslim" and until we can get past that we can't get to the table and talk about equality. Forget gender balance, we don't even have gender presence.' Some of the women believed there was no desire to fight sexism in Muslim communities because it is simply too patriarchal. Asma Barlas reported that 'Many Muslims recoil from it because it means challenging the system of male privilege that benefits so many men.' Likewise Malika said, 'It's not viewed as a priority by the community as a whole. Sexism is a social norm in the Muslim community, and it's framed as religious principles.' For Waajida, 'The day we know we have made progress towards equality in the Muslim world is the day men stop joking around about polygamy.'

Latifa feels that cultural attitudes are the biggest issue. When I asked her how she thought Australian Muslims viewed internal fighting of sexism, she said, 'By the established male hierarchy, it's viewed with huge suspicion. They have this idea of "We want to have control", particularly in the Arab community it's all about face, and that's based on his family. So if the wife is too outspoken, that reflects on him … It's a long road to go to carve out sexism.'

Those who believed there were differing opinions among Muslims towards fighting sexism identified various groups of people who were supportive or critical. Some said the split was along generational lines, whereas others felt the split was along gender lines. Asra is convinced that the division within Muslim communities concerning the fight against sexism comes down to differing understandings of what constitutes sexism in the first place, and particularly the role of 'benevolent sexism', as mentioned earlier. She explains, 'People think they're against sexism, and that it "honours" women to have a separate space, that it "honours" a woman to force or pressure her to cover up. They don't see how that's sexist. They think not having fair inheritance is okay because the man protects the woman. I think their definition of what's sexist is very different. I think these men and women would argue, "Hey, we're not being unfair—we're being fair-er. Look at the West, all these women have to work, at least we take care of our women." They don't think it's sexist to have a double standard about boys and girls, protecting a girl's honour more. I think the greatest challenge is not about sexism as a word, but double standards. I feel a lot of the community doesn't understand why a double standard isn't a good thing, how separate is not equal.'

Significantly, however, while there is by no means universal support for feminism in Western, non-Muslim societies, all of the women I interviewed thought non-Muslims are adamantly in favour of abolishing sexism among Muslims. Of the women who answered the question, less than one in five believed there were at least some non-Muslims who were able to view such action without racist or Islamophobic overtones. The vast majority believed non-Muslims saw fighting sexism within Muslim communities as very important, specifically because they felt that Islam is inherently sexist, that sexism is rife in Muslim communities, and that Muslim women were perpetual victims. As such, this support is often tainted by a fair degree of hypocrisy. As Asma Barlas put it, 'Many non-Muslims feel that sexism only exists in Muslim societies and they attack it with a self-righteousness which ignores that there is sexism and violence against women in their own communities.' Similarly, Jessica told me that, 'Non-Muslims like [to hear about us fighting sexism] but of course it is always in this context that Islam is the devil for women.'

The few women who believed there was some genuine understanding and goodwill in the non-Muslim community towards fighting sexism nonetheless acknowledged the existence of a pervasive attitude of female Muslim victimhood. As Ghayda told me, 'They either use our work to shore up stereotypes about our ethnicities or religion, or they understand there is a need.' Ify believed non-Muslims' attitudes towards the work they were doing could be divided into two groups, either complete rejection based on their belief that Islam was unchangeably sexist, or they were from other religious traditions, such as orthodox Judaism and Roman Catholicism, that had similarly wrestled with such work. Zafreen, on the other hand, didn't think non-Muslims were even capable of comprehending that fighting sexism among Muslims could occur, as illustrated by her comment, 'I think non-Muslims would be surprised or sceptical that that was even going on in our community.'

The existential and emotional turmoil in which the women are caught is very real, and often they find themselves in a double bind that presents a particular challenge to their efforts against sexism in Muslim communities.

Five
THE DOUBLE BIND

> I don't want to give ammunition to Islamophobes, but I can't remain silent if something needs to be corrected. But we need to be tactful and work quietly and persistently rather than being too outspoken and noisy about it.
>
> — *Karima*

With these two short sentences, Karima perfectly encapsulates the dual problem faced by women who fight sexism within Muslim communities—the concern not to provide fuel to Islamophobes, and the consciousness of a resistant, often-critical Muslim community—in their need, compulsion, even, to speak the truth about sexism. It is critical that these intersecting forms of discrimination, of sexism and control within the Muslim community, and the often-gendered Islamophobia in the wider community, are understood. What was revealed by the women I spoke with was that there were not just intersecting but competing forms of discrimination, and that the women had to constantly balance and re-negotiate them in their work fighting sexism.

These prejudices created a near-constant tension for many of my participants, as they regularly re-evaluated what they were doing and saying, who their audience was, and the potential cost–benefit of any statement (verbal or otherwise) they may make. Every public display came after an internal bargaining process. Some women judged that searing honesty about sexism among Muslims was always worth it despite the potential embarrassment and backlash, others were more circumspect and discerning. All of them had considered the idea, and none of them suggested they were surprised or thrown by my question on this double bind. It is undoubtedly a serious issue; Ghayda called it 'the biggest theoretical issue' because it involves 'walking a very fine line: you don't want to flame the fires of Islamophobia or alienate or ostracise Muslims, but you want to tell it like it is and bring up real concerns that Muslim women face.' Commentator Sara Khan looked frankly at the situation for Muslim women who encounter violent anti-Muslim attacks from racist bigots on the one hand, and sexism within Muslim communities, noting, 'some women refuse to speak out against gender-based discrimination fearing this would only fuel anti-Muslim hatred—of which they'd be the likely victims.'

Whether it is carefully selecting the right words or prefacing more critical remarks with positive anecdotes, the women found themselves in a state of perpetual balancing and bargaining. Not one of them said they were willing to lie or minimise, much less deny the reality of sexism in their communities, but many were also very reluctant to contribute to the negative perception about Islam that is already widespread among non-Muslims. They were often strongly motivated by a genuine desire to protect the religion they loved from more hostility and misunderstanding, and did not want to make other Muslims think they were throwing out the baby with the bathwater.

Because of the suspicion with which many Muslims view fighting sexism or anything that smacks of feminism, as well as the pervasive fear of 'airing dirty laundry', my participants had to be very wise with the words and examples they used in situations when speaking about sexism among Muslims, either to other Muslims or to non-Muslims. This poses particular challenges in a digital age, where most speeches and interviews are instantly available online for a global audience well beyond the speaker's intended audience. It is a situation that can be more debilitating, more censorious than even overt censorship. Some of the women I interviewed confessed to feeling that they were almost never able to speak in a truly open and authentic way. As Amina told me, 'I try to give a very nuanced rendition of the issues that are a concern to me, but what I usually find for me is most helpful is to know my audience. So before I get someplace I ask, "Who is the audience?" So I gear my presentations to different types of audiences in different ways ... I must locate my discussion, that is, give my definitions of Islam, I have to recognise the presence of Islamophobia, I have to recognise the presence of Wahabi-salafism, I have to recognise those things, locate my work relative to those things, and then make my comments. So by that time 45 minutes is up and I've got 15 minutes to actually make my point. Opportunities for me to take 45 minutes to say what I want are actually very rare ... And I accept that as part of the challenge. That's part of the challenge of being from the West and fully Muslim.'

This is obviously frustrating, particularly for a woman who defines herself primarily as a theologian who, above all else, values the creation and sharing of ideas; that is, she sees herself 'as a theologian who is an activist. I don't put them at the same level. I think I still give primacy to knowledge production ... It is necessary to challenge stasis in thinking and acting, and the challenge in the thinking is what holds us back as an *ummah*, I believe, so my priority is still in the area of knowledge production.' To feel so convinced about the stunting effect of 'unchallenged—that is, sexist—thinking' and to feel simultaneously constrained from adequately addressing it would be both exasperating and profoundly demoralising. Waajida also discussed the tension she felt in her dealings with non-Muslims and the way she almost has to engage in a kind of sophistry. 'Can you imagine if you open up to the wider community and told them we can't access our local mosque? It has happened, we hired a church facility for some years because we could not use the mosque, and the church leader said, "Don't you have a mosque around the corner?" What could I say? "Yeah, but they don't like hearing our voices!" … [T]hen I'm affirming and confirming the stereotypes. And our stereotypes are real. I want to say they're just stereotypes, but they're real. They're not real in that they're not true to Islam, but they are real. And that's when you don't want to come and tell the wider community because all this time we've been saying, "No, no what's happening in Saudi and Afghanistan that's not right, that's not Islam, that's not the way of the Prophet," but it's very real. There's injustice, there's sexism throughout the whole Muslim world and Muslim communities.'

Waajida's struggle, like Amina's, is compounded when we consider the way she defines herself. Much of Waajida's work is educating the wider, non-Muslim community and other Muslims (especially Muslim women) about Islam and, in particular, teaching about Islamic attitudes towards women. She told me, 'I'm passionate about women's rights; the other passion I have is Allah. And I realise they cannot be separated.' When Waajida so clearly identifies as someone who teaches non-Muslims about Islam, as well as working to protect women's rights within Muslim communities through a strong, passionate belief in the religion, her sense of contradiction, of the constraints of what she can and cannot say will, like Amina's, be felt acutely.

Asifa acknowledged that when addressing Muslims and non-Muslims alike, she constantly feels the need 'to address the positive as well as the negative in the same breath, so that you don't come out sounding like an apologist if you only say the positive and you have things used against you if you only use the negative'. And yet this is no argument for timidity. Asifa says that the argument she puts to the Muslim community is that the problem it has with sexism 'is no secret' from non-Muslims. 'They already know all of these things about us, so if I don't address it, it looks like I have my head in the sand about it, and I won't be taken credibly as a feminist or a scholar if I pretend like everything is rosy. So the idea that if you don't talk about it, they won't use it against you is a mistake because they're already using it against us. There's already a misunderstanding of the history, stories and law, so I think it's important for Muslims to be educated about the very painful stuff.'

Latifa offered a succinct, concrete example of the way Muslim women have to carefully manage Muslim sensibilities just as much as they do non-Muslim attitudes when confronting sexism. She described a conference she organised to tackle the way imams are limiting women's roles. The idea of the conference, she said, was to 'focus on the negative role that imams play in preventing women from working, and keeping them housebound and keeping them under the control of their husbands rather than encouraging them to develop themselves financially, educationally and so on. I was convinced that was the case.' In order to highlight this problem and begin to address it, Latifa said she 'decided to focus on the initiatives of women who have overcome that, and women who have gone out and done great things, and then got the *shaykhs* to comment as part of that. So in every case I try to turn it around and say, "How can we address this issue, and focus on doing something about it?"' Instead of loudly condemning the imams—which, no doubt, would have garnered the attention of the media—Latifa was tactful and gentle in her approach, giving the imams a stage but carefully orchestrating the scenario in which they spoke in order to get her desired outcome.

About half of the women fell into the category of feeling seriously hindered by the double bind, while the other half acknowledged its presence but forged ahead, undeterred, anyway. Significantly, the women I spoke with did not identify a single dominating force as more problematic in the competing prejudices. Both restriction and judgement from Muslims and Islamophobia and derision from the non-Muslim community came up in equal measure as debilitating factors, as well as their own personal commitment to their faith. It seemed to genuinely hurt some of the women I interviewed by having to acknowledge that the faith they viewed as more important than anything else was going to be viewed more negatively by non-Muslims if they were honest about sexism among Muslims. Beyond just feeling conflicted or impeded by the interplay between reinforcing Islamophobia and speaking the truth about sexism, they also had to contend with a strong, critical push from within Muslim communities. This involved urging the women to keep silent—not 'airing dirty laundry' was a common refrain from the women interviewed—or to deny the existence of the problem in their approach to the issue. An example of this was stating that the situation for women in mosques wasn't that bad or was in fact required by Islamic law, and that the women who were trying to change it were *fitna*-causing troublemakers. This meant that at best, the women weigh up the positives and negatives before speaking openly—still with the full knowledge they will have to deal with the negative ramifications from both the Muslim and wider communities—and, at worst, that women reconfigure their message into something less threatening, and thus less powerful, or become silent altogether when they decide the cost is just too high. The double bind definitely affects both categories of women, as all Muslim women are potential recipients of (often gendered) Islamaphobia from outside Muslim communities and (often gendered) censure within Muslim communities.

The double bind experienced by Muslim women is, of course, not a new phenomenon. At least as far back as the early twentieth century, Muslim women writers struggled with this concept. Zeyneb Hanoum, the Turkish woman who wrote her own, more accurate account of life in the harem, for example, grappled with knowing that her writing must appeal to a Western audience in order to gain traction and change what she saw as misinformation, but creating that appeal could easily turn her into an Orientalist object of fancy. Indeed, she wrote about her unease with being treated as a 'living spectacle' by women in France—a term that would probably be known today as 'the exotic other'. In a more modern account by Muslim women, academic Aysha Hidayatullah wrote openly of her anguish over publishing a highly critical account of Muslim feminist theology. She said she was 'all too aware of the tremendous risks associated with airing my critiques of feminist Qur'anic interpretations', knowing that she was 'supplying bigoted opponents of Islam with more fodder to fuel anti-Islam propaganda based on the ideological premise that Islam is irreconcilably misogynistic'. She felt this made them more available to criticisms that 'they may twist into weapons to further their racist assault on Muslims, buttressed by the imperialist campaigns of American and European state actors capitalising on widespread fears of Islam'. Thus, Muslim women have long been—and continue to be—highly conscious of the double bind that fastens them in ways that silence, constrict and torment.

'Double jeopardy' was the term first used in the 1970s in the midst of the feminist and civil rights movement to describe the intersection of the racism and sexism that black women experienced. Since then its sibling phrase—double bind—has also come into prominence. Academic Shakira Hussein describes it as 'the position of minority women who are told that they must decide between their dual identities'. While many minority women experience this in various ways, Muslim women most often find themselves caught 'between patriarchy and racism'. As social scientist Christina Ho puts it, it manifests itself for Muslim women when 'speaking out about oppressive practices in their own community, such as gendered violence, can result in being treated like a traitor by their own community, while also reinforcing negative stereotypes of the majority society of oppressive, backward cultures'.

As with black women, Muslim women's motivating force when choosing to speak out is always about receiving equity and justice—whether as Muslims or as women, or as both, for much of the sexism they are fighting against in Muslim communities derives from the conviction that their religious rights as women are being denied. Their pursuit of this goal becomes entangled when they are forced to choose between facilitating Islamophobia or angering their religious community. They feel they must choose between being open about sexism among Muslims and thereby risk 'fanning the flames' of Islamophobia and provoking the anger of Muslims, or remain silent, thus leaving sexism, discrimination and abuse within Muslim communities unaddressed and reinforcing the view that Muslim women are but silent, passive victims. Women in such a bind are often punished whichever choice they make.

Islamophobia often takes a specifically gendered form. Studies have shown the practical implications gendered Islamophobia has for Muslim women, such as the discrimination they face when seeking employment while in hijab and the higher reported incidence of identifiable Muslim women facing verbal and physical abuse on the streets of Western countries than Muslim men. It is therefore fair to say my participants' concerns about experiencing Islamophobia, as Muslims and especially as Muslim women, are real and valid. Indeed, often the fight against gendered Islamophobia can be an act of fighting sexism both inside and outside Muslim communities.

At this point, the way that American author and social activist bell hooks eloquently addressed the problem of the double bind—in this case, the bind posed by the prevalence of sexism and misogyny in the world of gangsta rap—is particularly instructive. In *Outlaw Culture*, she recounts her interview with Ice Cube, a rap artist with notoriously sexist lyrics, in which she did not adopt the critical, adversarial tone that the mainstream, white media had expected. As she describes it, 'when this interview came to press it was sliced to ribbons', because 'clearly folks at the magazine did not get the darky spectacle they were looking for'. She calls the whole affair 'a mass media set-up'. hooks did not approach her interview blithely ignorant of the misogyny Ice Cube and rappers like him peddle through their music, but she was keenly aware of the wider context in which young black men were and are operating, which in her words is one of 'white supremacist capitalist patriarchy'. hooks was by no means giving black men a free pass when it comes to sexism when she said, 'Black females must not allow ourselves to be duped into supporting shit that hurts us under the guise of standing besides our men'. She felt that if black men were betraying black women 'through acts of male violence', then the women must save themselves and those around them by resisting. 'Yet our feminist critiques of black males,' she added, 'fail as meaningful political interventions if they seek to demonize black males, and do not recognize that our revolutionary work is to transform white supremacist capitalist patriarchy where it is made manifest'.

She was not willing publicly to attack 'Brother Cube', as she called him, for the titillation of a mostly white mainstream media audience. But by spending most of the interview discussing 'the political, spiritual and emotional self-determination of black people', neither did she give the false impression that sexism was always the trump issue for her, a black woman. hooks was well aware of the double bind that the interview presented to her—no matter which approach she had taken, there would have been criticism from at least one interested party. Nonetheless, in her own inimitable way, she managed to refuse the terms of the choice itself.

This demand to choose also puts Muslim women in the unenviable position of offending a group from whom they already receive criticism, only then to be accused of betraying the cause—be it opposing Islamophobia or fighting sexism—to which they are deeply committed. It is important to note, however, that it is not only Muslim women who suffer from the treacherous terms of double bind; Muslim men experience it well, in the form of what has been called a 'double-bind of performativity'. This occurs when Muslims are expected to perform overt, and often extreme, demonstrations of allegiance to an adopted Western culture while at the same time needing or wanting to demonstrate religious allegiances (through religious dress or appearance, for example), and being pressured from competing communities to prioritise one loyalty over the other.

The problem of the double bind confronting Muslim women must be understood in the broader context of the manner in which Muslims are expected and allowed to engage non-Muslims in public conversation. This is a framework in which 'the stage is set and the script is already determined' as discussions are only to proceed when dictated by the 'interests and prejudices of a non-Muslim audience rather than the issues of most importance or relevance to Australian Muslims themselves' as media academic Tanja Dreher put it. When Muslims, and specifically Muslim women, are aware that their participation in public debate is acceptable only when it follows parameters set by a majority to whom they are seen as not belonging, this inevitably affects both the content and extent to which engagement is sought.

This is most visible whenever jihad and terrorism are the story of the day. Dreher found this in her research, where Australian Muslim women noted their discussions with journalists are framed in ways that wholly suit the journalist, such that 'We have had to explain jihad in a way that's been useful to them, as opposed to a way that's been useful to us'. This is one useful example of the way in which 'racialised communities learn the many ways in which their perspectives and priorities simply do not count as newsworthy'.[1]

I would suggest that the double bind experienced by Muslim women is ultimately constructed by the competing ways many Muslims and non-Muslims view each other, coupled with the gendered, sexist way both sides view Muslim women—either as oppressed/weak/victims by non-Muslims or as needing to be controlled and dismissed by Muslims. In the same way that Associate Professor of Sociology Deborah King identified that double jeopardy is in fact multiplied (not merely added) discrimination, and scholar Tricia Rose referred to it as 'negotiating multiple boundaries' for African-American female rappers, I argue that the double bind experienced by many Muslim women is 'multiplied control' by the non-Muslim community and those in the Muslim community; the impact of the criticism and control imposed by both Muslim and non-Muslim audiences has a multiplying—as opposed to just additional—effect. And it is this multiplied control that leads to an effective silencing—or, at very least, a curtailing of the speech—of Muslim women.

Half of the participants I interviewed found aspects of the double bind hindering in some way, and felt it infringed on the work they did and the reception they received—whether from Muslims, non-Muslims or both. The other half, however, felt differently. Acknowledging the idea of a double bind, they all made the conscious decision, for a variety of reasons, not to be confined by it. Some had reached the stage where they no longer cared if their words made Muslims look bad; others felt skirting around the truth negated the humanity of Muslim communities; while some still thought discussing problems openly actually made Muslims look more positive.

The first group of women who refused to be bound by the double bind often seemed frustrated and impatient at other Muslims' suggestion that 'airing dirty laundry in public' was something problematic and to be avoided. They clearly decided that speaking out was more important than concerns about community image or non-Muslim prejudice. As Asra put it, 'If people are going to hate on the faith, they're going to hate on it. So I hear that argument, but I have to admit I don't think about it much because I don't want it to be suffocating. I think for me, I don't care how the Muslim community looks. I have no protection of image. I don't fall for that at all, because I don't care.'

Hakimah was similarly candid about speaking openly regardless of how it made Muslims look or whether Muslims didn't like it. Both she and Asra were in professions—journalism and international diplomatic engagement amidst warfare, respectively—where they were required to speak openly and not gloss over negatives, irrespective of the cost. This sense of professional duty has clearly influenced Hakimah's approach: 'If I see something really horrible taking place, I won't not talk about it because I'm afraid of what that might do to the image of Muslims. I speak it the way I see it because that's the job I've been asked to do and the oath I took.' She went on to give an example of speaking openly about rampant sexual abuse of children in some Muslim countries. 'I have seen paedophilia in Muslim communities throughout the Gulf and in Afghanistan. It is prevalent; it is all over the place. [I feel it] is outrageous that we are not talking about what is happening to young boys. Mothers in Afghanistan told me that when the Taliban came to Afghanistan, they welcomed them because the Taliban told them that they would protect their sons who were being taken by the warlords on the way to school. Where is the conversation about that?'

For Adrienne, the refusal to be trapped by the double bind came from a very personal place. 'If the community is going to survive,' she said, 'then it cannot hide its abuses. Abuse can continue only when everyone is keeping it a secret "in the family". Also coming out of an abusive marriage and its secrecy meant I won't be secret about anything anymore and extend the violence in our community.'

Tayyibah's situation was somewhat different. She enjoyed the benefit of a mostly sympathetic female Muslim audience.

Knowing that she and her audience occupied a similar mental and spiritual plane gave her some enviable freedom in how she framed her arguments. 'I'm not writing … for the non-Muslim or Muslim men or the politician, but specifically for Muslim women who hold Islam dear … And I make sure that *Azizah* is a reflection of who Muslim women in America are. It's not a how-to-be-a-Muslim-woman book, it's what Muslim women in America are doing and saying and thinking and accomplishing. It's not about giving a utopic view of Islam, or to talk about Islam the way I practice it. We go to great lengths to be inclusive, we have different *madhahib* [schools of thought in Islamic jurisprudence], experiences, points of view. We try to talk about issues that impact community, such as betrayal in the last issue [of the magazine] for women who found out their husbands were cheating on them. It's not airing our dirty laundry—this is an issue for Muslim women and we're dealing with it, and that's part of it.'

Tayyibah shows the freedom a Muslim woman can experience, how unbound she can feel, when the pressure of appeasing a hostile non-Muslim audience is absent. Knowing that she is only, specifically targeting a Muslim female audience with a similar view of Islam as herself—women who have a deep, personal commitment to the faith—means she can unreservedly discuss issues of sexism within Muslim communities with the nuance she desires and without the need for qualifying reassurances. Comparing her situation and feelings to Amina's or Waajida's is a stark reminder that for those who feel trapped by the double bind—the impact is huge, and hinders their work significantly.

For women like Ingrid and Laleh, however, being open without fear of repercussions came from a place of truthfulness and authenticity. They correctly point out that the issues of sexism raised about Muslim communities are not uniquely Muslim issues but are in fact human issues, which affect nearly every group and religion on the planet. Ingrid insisted that it is not 'expressing solidarity to the community' when you refuse to confront injustice. 'The prophetic teaching that inspires me said "help your brother if he's being oppressed or the oppressor". We need to stop him doing the injustice, and it applies to all situations, but also in domestic violence. The wife isn't doing her husband any favours by allowing him to accumulate sins by allowing him to [abuse her].' Laleh concurred with Ingrid, highlighting that these are human issues that needed to be addressed as such—'Christian, Jewish, Hindu, atheist, whatever—they beat their wives. So domestic violence is across the wider community.'

For Asma Uddin and Daisy, expressing the diversity of opinions and a preparedness to address the sexism that occurs within Muslim communities trumped any pressure felt by the double bind, and they were both strong proponents of speaking honestly about issues to the wider community. As Asma said when thinking about her approach on AltMuslimah, 'The double bind definitely crosses my mind but showing an openness and more importantly, a solution to these problems, is infinitely better than putting up a front and trying to portray the community as perfect. You just have to be real, and show the full diversity.' Daisy takes this one step further, and argues that the double bind actually helps: 'The wider community thinks the Muslim community is a monolith … they think there's no internal dialogue and no critical thinking, we're just a bunch of monotonous, robotic people who think the same way and the only thing we want to do is bring shariah and stoning to this country. That's it. I have noticed that the most disarming thing for Americans is to say, "We have a problem. And yes, in certain countries and certain cultures women are very badly mistreated and we have to change that. But we Muslims have to be the ones to deal with it. And you have to allow us to do it … It's my job, I have to fix my own problems, fix my own extremists, you can't fix them, I can fix them." I have noticed that speaking openly about these issues is a relief for most Americans, and that we shouldn't be afraid to raise these issues.'

Clearly, the women I interviewed have very different feelings about the nature and impact of the double bind. For a significant number, it was a major hindrance imposed by both Muslim and non-Muslim communities. For others, it was just another obstacle to be overcome in their work. And for one, it was even viewed positively. I have experienced this myself numerous times in speeches, media engagements, and even personal interactions. I have rapidly evaluated where the greatest damage would result from my observations on sexism within the Muslim community, while still wanting to speak with integrity. Every time, I am aware there is no cost-free way to publicly address the issue, and so it is simply a matter—often with just a split-second to calculate during a live interview—of aiming for an acceptable balance of honesty and disclosure with minimal fallout.

It is also necessary to highlight that much of the discussion on the double bind and multiplied control identified here rests on the privileging of a non-Muslim audience's perspective in any discussions by and about Muslims. That many of the women in my study were aware and even anxious about how what they said could be used against them or their co-religionists by non-Muslims, to the extent that they modified or even halted their public discussion on topics that were very important to them, shows the powerful way in which the non-Muslim voice was favoured as the norm. Even the Muslim contribution to the double bind (criticising the Muslim women who spoke openly as 'airing dirty laundry', etc.) was predicated on the belief that the non-Muslim perception would be negatively influenced by disclosure and that that perception was paramount. While some of my participants understood the dominant power the non-Muslim opinion had and proceeded anyway out of a conviction to truth, there was an understandable pragmatism in the attitude of my participants who conceded to it in myriad ways that

I could not criticise; like it or not, non-Muslim perception *was* the standard on which conversation operated, and to pretend otherwise was disingenuous and even potentially dangerous. Whether the women I spoke with felt frustratingly constrained by the double bind, or were aware of its existence but felt it was not the trump card in their work, all were conscious of it in their fight against sexism.

Six
THE THIRD WAY: FAITH AND FEMINISM

> At the outset it should be made clear—as history and empirical research attest—that the feminisms Muslim women have created are feminisms of their own. They were not 'Western'; they are not derivative.
>
> — *Margot Badran*

Islam is not unique in having androcentric theological interpretations. Christian, Jewish and Buddhist women (and men) have grappled with the overt and covert sexism within their own sacred texts and traditions, and have negotiated the area in numerous ways. This is because religion is made up of people and, sadly, where there are people there is often sexism. Sexism within societies is frequently echoed by, and transplanted onto numerous social institutions, such as the law and politics. As sociologist Andrew Singleton explains, 'Because most societies are traditionally patriarchal, religious organisations are as well.' We cannot help but bring our own biases and experiences to the world we interpret, and when religious texts are viewed through the sexist (or racist or pacifist or neo-liberal or pluralist or anything else) lens of the reader, the outcome is obvious.

There is a saying among Muslims: you don't read the Qur'an, the Qur'an reads you. This means that holy texts have a way of drawing out from people what already dwells in their hearts and holding up a mirror to them. This is not to say that there aren't valid and invalid interpretations of the Qur'an—classical Muslim scholars have spent generations discussing and debating where legitimate boundaries of interpretations lie, and there are most certainly readings that are classified as taking people outside the fold of Islam. However, if you have ever wondered how the Persian poet Rumi and the leader of the Islamic State can belong to the same religion and claim to follow the same scripture, this is a significant part of the reason.

As the scriptures of many religions have been used to either empower or crush women, Muslims today are facing a similar struggle. What would be surprising to scores of people, however, is that many Muslims see the Qur'an and *hadith* as a defence for their arguments against sexism, not as a stumbling block to women's liberation. For many of these Muslims, it is not merely about stamping out misogyny; fighting gender injustice is itself a religious act because sexism dishonours Islam. As one of the women I interviewed, Asma Barlas, previously wrote, 'What disturbs me most about misogyny in Muslim societies is not so much that it has been normalised or even that it has been wrapped in the mantle of religion; neither tendency, after all, is peculiar to Muslims. Rather, what I find intolerable is that Muslims project misogyny onto the scripture, hence onto the divine, on the basis of three or four words or phrases in the Qur'an, overlooking the egalitarian nature of the text as a whole.'

Believing that the treatment of women in Islam does not point to an inherent problem with Islam itself but is instead far more of a social phenomenon, Asma went on to state bluntly why she thinks things are the way they are. She said, 'The reasons Muslims have read the Qur'an as a patriarchal text has to do with who reads it (basically men), the contexts in which they have read it (basically patriarchal), and the method by which they have read it (basically one that ignores the hermeneutic principles that the Qur'an suggests for its own reading).' Implicit within this criticism is the solution she offers: re-reading the texts from a female perspective, within a pro-female framework, and with a whole-of-Qur'an hermeneutical approach—that is using the Qur'an to help explain itself, and being guided by the manifest overarching themes present in the book. But beyond that is something more obvious and profound: the Qur'an, and thus the Islamic faith, has within it sufficient resources to counter the sexism Muslim women face.

I was particularly interested in speaking to the women about the role faith has played in their fight against sexism. As well as wondering about it as a factor in their motivations and challenges, I felt it was also critical for three reasons: because of the belief that sexism is inherent to Islam, because of the belief that secular feminism is the only or best way to tackle sexism within the Muslim community, and because of the belief that fighting sexism within the Muslim community is new and antithetical to authentic Islamic teachings.

One of the central criticisms directed at the sexism experienced by Muslim women is that such sexism is inherent to Islam. That is, any sexism Muslim women experience within the Muslim community occurs because it is theologically required or, at the very least, endorsed. The accounts of certain individuals—generally female, ex-Muslims—of their Muslim upbringings and the misogynistic trials they endured and, finally, escaped, have become a best-selling sub-genre. Newspapers abound with horrifying stories about Muslim women being denied the right to drive, being forced to undergo female genital mutilation, or being stoned for being raped, with Islamic beliefs often cited as the cause. Such pervasive accounts cement in the public's mind that Islam is a religion that is actively misogynist.

Contrary to these grim accounts by outsiders, many Muslim women seem to have a different attitude. In a comparative study between American, religious Christian and Muslim women, researchers found that 'it was typical for Muslim women to report that their religion supported feminism and, interestingly, it was typical of Christian women to report that their religion does not support feminist ideals'. They also found that, 'Most of the Christian women in this study rejected the label of feminist, but espoused feminist values. In contrast, most of the Muslim women were willing to endorse the label of feminist, and actually identified Islam as a feminist religion.' More tellingly, still, 'The majority of Muslim women identified as feminist. This finding is in stark contrast to the common perception of Muslim women in American society.' These conclusions are echoed by many of my participants—even if they do not all subscribe to the word feminist, they still felt it had an inherently anti-sexist core—and it is telling that these results were deemed so surprising.

The belief that secular feminism is the only way to approach gender reform in the Muslim community does not just come from non-Muslims. Many Muslims also assume that any endeavour to eradicate sexism within Muslim communities must draw from the wells of secular feminism itself. This imposes a particular challenge to those women who want to fight against sexism within the Muslim community and who are already feeling under attack from non-Muslims: the allegation that they are doing something un-Islamic, that they are bringing in an approach that is foreign—and thus unacceptable—to the faith, and that they are not authentic, pious Muslims.

There is a significant degree of Muslim suspicion concerning secular feminism and this attitude can contribute to the binary of secular women's rights versus authentic Islam, just as greatly as non-Muslims' attitudes. As Margot Badran has demonstrated, 'Orientalist notions first articulated around the turn of the twentieth century and echoed later in the century by mainstream Islamists, both [contend] that Muslim women "cannot possibly be feminists".' Indeed, local, indigenous feminisms in many countries have been well-documented for some time, and 'yet despite a large literature in many languages recording and critiquing these globally scattered feminisms, the notion that feminism is Western is still bandied about by those ignorant of history—or who perhaps wilfully employ it as a delegitimizing tactic'. The pressure from Muslims and non-Muslims alike to consider oneself either a 'proper' Muslim or someone who fights actively against sexism is what participant Asifa Quraishi has called a 'false dichotomy', where 'one must be either "pro-Islam" or "pro-women" but not both' in her legal journal article. Such a false choice is not only intellectually superficial, but denies the reality of many Muslim women who successfully combine strong personal commitment to their faith with a commitment to gender justice, and who seek this justice as the very expression of their faith.

The women I interviewed who reject this binary embody, what I call, a 'third way', or an alternative to the dichotomy that is forced upon them. Badran calls it 'a middle space, or independent site, between secular feminism and masculinist Islamism', and goes on to argue that, 'Islamic feminism transcends and eradicates old binaries. These include polarities between "religious" and "secular" and between "East" and "West".' Nevertheless, for a variety of reasons, some women reject the label 'feminist' for themselves or the work they do, and this is a legitimate choice to make. Muslim women who fight against sexism without that label are the tree that falls in the patriarchal forest regardless of an audience—their work continues, and the sound it makes is irrelevant.

Of my participants, the vast majority adamantly identified as 'religion-positive' or working from within a religious paradigm in their efforts to fight sexism in Muslim communities. This is most significant when considered in the light of common belief that Islam is inherently sexist and disadvantageous to women. The women in this section are a good mix of ages, cultural backgrounds and education levels, and yet they all responded with similar vehemence, which is a powerful response to the common rhetoric levelled at them.

Tayyibah affirmed that she sees herself as 'definitely pro-faith' and that she regards Islam as her 'spiritual and moral compass'. She felt Islam contains 'solutions for any problems that humanity is experiencing'. Likewise, Waajida points to the Prophet's establishment of the requirements of fairness, equality, justice, mercy and compassion: 'For me teaching from a faith perspective is very powerful. It's actually more powerful than any other perspective, any other "ism" or creating an institution of any kind. Because it goes to the heart of a person, it changes them.' Zafreen, too, insisted that such a religious approach was superior to secular feminism: 'Islam and its teachings are capable of giving women an equal footing in society to men, and that Islam does not relegate women to the private sphere. I really believe some Muslims have distorted our teachings and forgotten our heritage. I believe that Islam can be used as a source of empowerment for women. I believe that. I don't need to rely on Germaine Greer or a secular model in order to reclaim my dignity as a woman. Islam can give me that.' For Umaymah, there is no conflict between feminism and Islam; rather, 'there's a correlation, not a conflict'.

Other women I spoke with felt differently. Asifa and Ghayda, for example, both felt that they drew equally from a religious and secular feminism framework in their work, where appropriate. Ghayda confessed that she does not believe that 'all problems can be solved within an Islamic framework because not all problems are strictly Islamic'. Nonetheless, she also believes that 'Islam is being reinterpreted in dynamic ways that make it applicable to problems in predominantly Muslim countries.' Asifa is more circumspect, when explaining how and why she switches between approaches depending on her audience.

'If I'm speaking to a completely secular feminist audience, I'm not going to be making Islamic law, faith-based arguments for general topics like women's education or leadership. But if I'm speaking to an audience where I know this might be a stumbling block for them for religious reasons, then I need I take on those religious reasons ... So then I would speak from a more pro-faith perspective explicitly. Even though my own internal personal dynamic is probably going to be very influenced by pro-faith stuff as well as secular feminist and international human rights stuff. So, for example, if I'm thinking about women's access to education, I could quote the declaration on human rights, or the Platform for Action for Women written for the 1995 [CEDAW] conference, but for someone like my dad, who is a very strong practising Muslim, who has a lot of scepticism about Western neo-colonialism, that wasn't going to get very far to get him to let me go away to college. He didn't care for that stuff. But if I quoted the Qur'anic verse that said it is incumbent on every Muslim male and female to seek knowledge, now I have his attention. So that's the kind of thinking that would be part of my tool box when there's some issue on the ground that I want to effect, whether it's change or just empowerment in general. It really has to do with effective accomplishment of the goal.

'In many cases—not all, but in many cases—the goals are the same, whether you're coming from a pro-faith perspective or a secular feminist perspective. Nobody wants women to be imprisoned or punished because they were victims of rape [referring to the situation in Pakistan where rape victims were jailed if they could not produce four witnesses to their attack]. Nobody does, nobody in their right minds wants that. So if a Western feminist comes in and tries to attack the *hudud* laws that are being used to do this, the pushback you're getting isn't because someone wants these rape victims to be punished. That would be a skewing of their perspective. What they want is for Islamic law to be respected and to be honoured in their society. And at some point along the way they've been convinced that that is what it is. But when you really show them the sources and say, "Look at this," they realise that it's not it. And that's what happened in Pakistan. They actually had the Muslim scholars there themselves saying, "This is not what Islam teaches," and that took down the intensity of the defence in the public of these laws that are extremely harmful on a human rights basis but also on an Islamic basis. So when I published my article on *zina* [adultery or pre-marital sex] in Pakistan, the introduction is different than the version here. The introduction here [in the Western copy] is, "This is an interesting topic, let's think about this." There [in Pakistan] it's, "You are harming Islam by having this law in the books. It isn't good for us as Muslims and it's not good for Islam to have these kinds of laws because it's not our law and you're calling it our law and that's causing harm." So understanding your audience, understanding how to make your argument, that's where the pro-faith versus pro-secular approach matters to me.'

It is worth pointing out that Asifa's approach is neither anomalous nor historically unusual. In fact, there is a long history of Muslim women who work in the area of gender justice utilising both secular and religious arguments as appropriate, despite arguments of conflict or incompatibility. As Badran argues, any suggestions 'or allegations of a supposed "clash" between "secular feminism" and "religious feminism" may result from ignorance—or, more likely, from a politically motivated attempt to impede solidarities among women'. She says secular feminism, which is frequently just called feminism, 'offered Islamic arguments in demanding women's rights to education, work, political rights—along with secular nationalistic, humanitarian (later human) rights, and democratic arguments'. So that when changes 'to the Muslim personal status code' were pleaded for, 'they advanced Islamic arguments'.

In certain circumstances—Egypt in the early twentieth century being the prime example—Muslim women using secular approaches to feminism did not necessarily mean a feminism devoid of religious consideration in the way that it is now commonly understood. Instead, their use of secularism was a way to embrace both Muslim and Coptic Christian (the largest religious minority in Egypt) women within the group's endeavours, and to tackle both public and private forms of sexism using different tools, including Islamic sacred texts. This suggests that, at least historically, the divide between religious and secular approaches to feminism or fighting sexism was less pronounced than it is today.

The women who subscribe to a faith-positive and faith-grounded approach to their fight against sexism are often not simply doing so from a personal belief that this is an Islamic imperative, but also for pragmatic reasons: a faith-centred and Islamically authentic approach to tackling sexism within Muslim communities is much more likely to be effective than any exogenous means. As American scholar of Islam Kecia Ali explains in her book *Sexual Ethics and Islam*, for most Muslims, 'whether a particular belief or practice is acceptable' depends on 'whether or not it is legitimately "Islamic"'. This, she says, is true of Muslims everywhere, even if they considered themselves moderate or progressive, extremists or conservatives. 'Even many of those who do not base their personal conduct or ideals on normative Islam believe, as a matter of strategy, that in order for social change to achieve wide acceptance among Muslims they must be convincingly presented as compatible with Islam.' Furthermore, she feels, 'This focus on Islamic authenticity is particularly intense on matters relating to women, gender and the family.'

Religious currency is crucial if the work is to have any traction within Muslim communities. Laleh whole-heartedly agreed, saying, 'Irshad Manji and Ayaan Hirsi Ali, they're not going to change the Muslim community. Ever. But if you work from within the community and you believe in it and you love it as much as [other Muslims] do, then they understand your sincerity, and they really look into what you're saying.' Such religious currency is especially important for women, as Azizah Al-Hibri, founder and president of K.A.R.A.M.A.H.: Muslim Women Lawyers for Human Rights, insists when she says it 'is important to keep in mind that most Muslim women tend to be highly religious and would not want to act in contradiction to their faith'. This is because any 'conflict created by patriarchal interpretations for Muslim women who do not have the benefit of a religious education is frightening'. She goes on to say that 'the majority of Muslim women who are attached to their religion will not be liberated through the use of a secular approach imposed from the outside by international bodies or from above by undemocratic governments'. There is just one way to resolve the conflicts of these women, she says, to 'remove their fear of pursuing rich and fruitful lives is to build a solid Muslim feminist jurisprudential basis, which clearly shows that Islam not only does not deprive them of their rights, but in fact demands these rights for them'.

The vast majority of the women I interviewed did not feel their religion was inherently sexist, and actually believe it to be the most effective tool to challenge and change the sexism within Muslim communities. They attributed any sexist beliefs among Muslims to either patriarchal interpretations of religious texts by men or widespread ignorance of the unadulterated teachings of their faith. This idea of a genuine faith that needs to be excavated to uncover its egalitarian bedrock was something to which several of the women I interviewed alluded. Here Nahida spoke about feminism being one of the key reasons for divine revelation in Islam and the need to reclaim religious texts previously used for women's oppression: 'I am definitely of the perspective that religion is the key to liberating women—that feminist purpose was its very objective in revelation. Religion does not belong to men, it simply needs to be reclaimed by women to be employed for the very cause that it was introduced: to free the oppressed and bring peacefulness and goodness. One of the most important tools are useable resources—aspects of the religion, texts or practices, that when rightfully seized by women once more enable women to reacquire the rights that were given to them by God from the very beginning.'

Such a belief asserts that the core faith doesn't need reform or radical change, but is instead simply being misconstrued. This means there is no challenge to divine authority but instead a criticism of the imperfect (mostly male) humans who interpret it. This is an important distinction, as it shows there is no attack on the holiness or infallibility of the Qur'an or its teachings by the women I interviewed. Such an attack could have the serious consequence of them being viewed as apostates, as Abdullahi An-Na'im, an expert in Islam and human rights, highlights when she says, 'To attribute inadequacy to any part of Shari'a is regarded as heresy by the majority of Muslims, who believe that the whole of Shari'a is divine.' He feels that the 'first step in overcoming this obstacle is to show that the public law of Shari'a is not really divine law in the sense that all its specific principles and detailed rules were directly revealed by God to the Prophet Muhammad'. He also says that Muslims 'may become more willing to accept the possibility of substantial reform ... If it can be shown that Shari'a was constructed by the early Muslim jurists out of the fundamental sources of Islam, namely the Qur'an and Sunna.'

As a result, for these women the way of tackling gender justice through religious sources that for so long have been used for patriarchal ends does not equate to disregarding these sources, but approaching them with the intention of reinterpreting them. They argue that they can do this, because until now, the majority of what we understand to be Islamic is little more than a masculine overlay. As academic Amal Treacher says, our societies are constructed on a patriarchal model. That is, our political and social systems are controlled by men, and this has led to the distortion of the teachings of the Qur'an. The true meanings within the Qur'an and *hadith* are construed in such a way that women are oppressed. 'A return to the word of the Qur'an, the *hadith*, and the *Shari'a* is the way forward.'

When I asked Asma Barlas about the approach she uses in her work, she spoke about this issue of competing interpretations and the primacy of working within an Islamic framework. 'For a believer,' she says, 'scripture provides the moral and ethical framework for living a good life and it seems reasonable to assume that Muslims will look to the Qur'an for guidance in living their lives. The problem arises when we are told that only certain interpretations of its teachings are the "real" Islam. One can only push against this idea from within an Islamic framework. This doesn't mean that simply adopting what you call a "pro-faith" perspective is enough. After all, many Muslim "fundamentalists" also adopt such a perspective. What is important is to question definitions of faith that encode the notion of male privilege as a God-given right. How can one do any of this from "outside" an Islamic framework?'

While my focus has been on Muslim women labouring in North American and Australian contexts, it is important to note that, within the body of global Muslim women, the use of Islam to challenge sexism from a pragmatic framework is being done by women who do so because they have no other choice. That is, it is not a combination of personal conviction in Islam plus recognition of the practical benefit of using religious arguments, but instead a case of women who must operate with an Islamic political context and thus have no other option but to utilise religious arguments. This is the situation of many women gender activists in Iran, for example. The nature of Iranian society and the primacy of Islam as the political system mean that they have no choice but to operate within a religious framework in their activities. It is important that this reality be highlighted, not only to emphasise the unique and more autonomous situation in which the women I spoke with operate, but to give a fuller picture of the global situation of Muslim women fighting sexism.

Two of the women I interviewed raised similar stories about their journey to reconcile their faith with their commitment to gender justice. Both spoke of how they were initially made to feel there was an unbridgeable gap between Islam and the struggle against sexism, and how they had to work through those issues to come to a point with which they felt reconciled. Research Fellow at Cornell University Nimat Barazangi identifies this phenomenon in her work, pointing to the tension many Muslim women experience 'because they were erroneously made to believe that males' interpretations are as binding as the Qur'anic principles themselves'.

This forced demarcation had a profound effect on Ayesha and Amina and the way they defined themselves. In the past, Amina said, 'we were forced to choose—either Islam or human rights. And of course all the secular feminists went with human rights and said, "we'll do without Islam", and all the Islamists took Islam and said, "we'll do without human rights", and there we were in the middle with no name and no program. And at this point now we've managed to make a program, an agenda, a methodology, an epistemology, written books and the position is: we do not accept either/or at all. We have to have full human rights and Islam and that's what you call pro-faith feminism.'

When I asked Amina to elaborate on this term 'pro-faith' and how it connects to her work on sexism within Muslim communities, she told me, 'I made a point of identifying as pro-faith because of my encounter with secular Muslim feminists; I realised that it was necessary to define what I mean by what I'm doing so that there was no confusion ... I used the term "pro-faith" but that was before the methodological articulations of Islamic feminism were coherent. Now they are much more coherent so I would go with "Islamic feminist", not "Muslim feminist"—because anybody can be Muslim and feminist—but an Islamic feminist, which is actually a methodology, it is a pro-faith perspective on gender reform. I can say that now, but I refused to say that for many, many years. Instead I gave myself a very long-winded title of "Pro-faith, pro-feminist".' Amina's remarks demonstrated the scholarly evolution in the Muslim community on gender issues in the last ten years. While, as she said, not everyone is on the same page, she felt the discussion has advanced adequately for her to publicly, confidently label herself an 'Islamic feminist'.

Ayesha also spoke of the process of her own reconciliation with both Islam and feminism through greater immersion in religious texts: 'It was my own personal epiphany ... because for a long time I did feel like feminism and Islam were different. And I was told you could only be secular if you were a feminist, you couldn't really have anything to do with Islam or any other religion. But once I started reading the mystical poets and reading a lot more about women who were deeply integrated into the Islamic tradition and yet were fighting for the rights of women, it started coming together for me, and giving me a living example of that and positive example of that.'

Amina and Ayesha both spoke compellingly about the journey towards creating what I have called a third way, and the vital importance of being able to define one's position on faith and women's rights for oneself. Amina and Ayesha, and all the women in my study, as Muslims who all reside in Western countries, represent a way to fight sexism that is influenced by both their Islamic religious heritage and their Western environments, and in this way they are helping to contribute towards new extensions of feminism. Feminism as a movement is ever evolving and is always a response to the sexism women experience. The methods of, and reasoning for, fighting sexism that the women in my study employ can fall under the heading of 'third-wave feminism', which is noted for respecting aspects of self, such as religion and race, but also 'allows for identities that previously may have been seen to clash with feminism', as Leslie Heywood notes, such as religious identities. Indeed, the first documented use of the term third wave was by Jacqui Alexander, Lisa Albrecht and Mab Segrest in the anthology 'The Third Wave: Feminist perspectives on racism in the 1980s', and specifically addressed the racial biases found in second-wave feminism.

Similarly, Chela Sandoval, a post-colonial feminist theorist, identified very early the diversity of opinion and experience that would be both unique and crucial to third-wave feminism, stating 'differential consciousness is vital to the generation of a next third wave women's movement and provides grounds for alliance with other decolonizing movements for emancipation'. Such comments helped solidify the growing perception of third-wave feminism's rejection of the 'essentialism, universalism and naturalism' of second-wave feminism. The fluidity of emerging third-wave feminism can allow for the types of feminism or approaches to gender justice that my participants demonstrate, and in turn, the work and beliefs of my participants can inform new understandings of the reach and possibility of third-wave feminism.

Finally, one of the women I interviewed claimed to operate solely from a secular feminist perspective. While only one of my participants did this, I think it is important to include this alternative approach to display the diversity and not give the false impression there was unanimity among the women on this topic. Asra admitted that she doesn't bear 'much hope for religion as an entity', and that this distance is reflected in the way she is raising her child. She says she still has 'hope inside the faith, but I see the real-life short-comings to such a degree in the community that I don't trust it to surrender my child to or my own well-being to, so I just try to carve my own spiritual, religious path'. Asra's decision to operate from a secular feminist perspective while still utilising the faith in order to effect change is by no means unique in Muslim communities today, nor is it unusual in the history of feminism in Muslim communities. However, it must be noted, once again, that within my sample of participants, she was the only one who had adopted such an approach.

Sadly, religion in general, and Islam in particular, are still viewed by many as inherently bound up with the problem of patriarchy. And yet faith can also play a significant role for women in the way they feel about and confront sexism. In their research on the ways religious Christian and Muslim women understood the connection between feminism and faith, Ali and colleagues argue that:

> It is true that for some women, religion may be negatively associated with patriarchy, oppression of women's rights, and intolerance. Yet, a lack of attention to the positive aspects of religion in women's lives denies a deeper understanding of women who may embrace strong religious values and the potential empowerment they may gain from their religion. Additionally, an automatic assumption of the disempowerment that religious women face does not allow for a full understanding of the role that feminism plays or can play in the lives of deeply religious women.

While much of the non-Muslim world appears dismissive of the value Islam can have in Muslim women's lives—and truly aghast at the notion it could play any role in eradicating the sexism in Muslim communities—the women I interviewed demonstrate otherwise. For them, Islam is a crucial tool in the work of gender justice and, in many instances, is the only realistic option for transformation. While some are proudly feminist and others more befitting of the de facto feminist label (if any label must be applied at all), these women have shown how they further develop and exist within the third way—regardless of the disapproval of other Muslims or non-Muslims. This third way, then, offers an important reciprocal relationship to third-wave feminism, both falling under it, and contributing to it.

CHANGING THE NARRATIVE

I was exasperated and weary when I began this project. I felt I could not endure one more non-Muslim's smug ignorance when pontificating about my faith and women's place within it. I felt I could not endure any more sexist situations within the Muslim community where change often seemed to move at glacial speed and the egalitarian spirit of my faith was ignored. And most of all, I couldn't take one more person's—Muslim or non-Muslim—suggestion that to want to eradicate sexism within the Muslim community, I and the women like me were 'bad Muslims', operating outside the faith and its tradition; that we could either be good Muslims or care about sexism, but never both. I desperately wanted to shift the needle—even slightly—on a record that had been stuck on the same, screeching track for decades.

I knew there were lots of other Muslim women engaged in this work, but it seemed very few outside the Muslim community knew they were, and sometimes it seemed that those within the Muslim community dismissed them as 'secular' or 'modernist', as opposed to the practising Muslim women they were. The experiences of the women I interviewed do not discount the experiences of other Muslim women: those who aren't particularly interested in, or have the capacity to, fight sexism; those who fight sexism, but do not use religion as a tool or motivator in their fight; those who do indeed see Islam as part of the problem. All these women can and do exist alongside the women I spoke to and those like them. They always have and probably always will. Yet while the voices of the indifferent or the incapable or the hostile or the otherwise focussed are heard, they often seemed to drown out the women like those in my investigation. But truth has many parts; none more important than the others. And each deserves attention.

For a project that was borne out of such frustration, it was immensely uplifting to undertake. I spent hours listening to inspiring women talk about their work, their motivations, how they just kept trying to implement change despite the many obstacles they encountered, and their passionate commitment to their faith. The women roared with laughter and they cried so hard they couldn't speak as they answered my questions. They were fearless and tireless.

At a time when I felt I was trudging through an unchanging desert of sexist and bigoted assumptions with no relief in sight, my conversations with these women about what it meant to be a Muslim woman and truly implement *shariah* in their lives, revitalised me. The word *shariah* literally means 'way to the watering place'—it's the path to a source of constant refreshment. And talking to these women was like a cool drink on my parched soul. In so many ways, these women have been my guides through harsh terrain.

The women here embody a new type of feminism, or gender consciousness in the West, one that embraces passionate religious attachment and conviction, while at the same time challenging sexism in ways that have coherence and currency in a modern, plural Western context. It is a third way that shatters long-standing dichotomies of religious Muslim woman and secular feminist. They were imaginative and constructive with what they were doing—pray-in protests in mosques, feisty tumblrs, and glossy lifestyle women's magazines all sat comfortably alongside deeply researched theological treatises and classes on spiritual discipline. It is a feminism that may not even adhere itself to such a name, and yet—or perhaps, because of that—falls within the fluid terrain of third-wave feminism. It is a responsive movement that is acutely influenced by expectations from both the Muslim and non-Muslim communities. This can be positive, such as the high level of support reported from Muslim males, and negative, such as the intense criticism. Given the projected development of Muslim communities in locations like North America and Australia, it will only continue to grow. The push for gender equality is a significant aspect of the rapidly growing Muslim communities in the West, and will no doubt continue to have potency not just for the local communities in which it finds itself, but the global *ummah*.

These stories of the women contribute to a new and much-needed understanding of Muslim women in minority contexts who engage in the work of fighting sexism within their own communities. That so many of my participants claimed a religious heritage to this work, and used this legacy as their platform for their efforts, also helps to develop a new understanding of Islam in a modern context, countering the dominant opinion of Islam as synonymous with repression and archaic thinking. Their insistence that not only was gender equality their God-given right but that their actions to achieve it were consistent with generations of pious Muslim women, was a powerful response to common perceptions of Islamic treatment of women, and offers an altered imaging of what it means to be a Muslim woman today.

The high level of intimacy and trust these women gave when sharing their personal stories, feelings, beliefs and struggles with me were based on our shared identity as Muslim women. They knew I was acutely empathetic to the conflicting and at times attacking domains in which they operated as well as someone who would not dismiss or belittle their religious convictions. The responses I was given were authentic, honest and very raw. I also had access to some well-known, highly respected and sometimes controversial women in the Muslim community, who are leaders in fighting sexism, adding not just a level of gravitas to the information but also building another layer of significance to the recording of detailed life stories of these trail-blazers. That two of the most accomplished, influential and spearheading women who participated died during the course of this book reinforces the importance of their accounts and perspectives, and also provides a very useful snapshot at a time when Muslim women are under significant political and media scrutiny.

Some findings were surprising: that Muslim men were named as some of the biggest supporters of the women I spoke to and that they reported more encouragement than discouragement from the Muslim community for the work they do. Likewise the overall premise, that of Muslim women fighting sexism from a faith-positive perspective, was counter-intuitive to many and not only helped to challenge the unrelenting stereotypes that circulate about Muslims and sexism but offered concrete research as proof against it.

Negative, condescending attitudes towards Muslim women abound in Western discussions, as does disbelief that fighting sexism within Muslim communities exists. Muslim women have been fighting sexism within their own communities from a faith-based perspective for a long time—as long as Islam has been around—and for nearly as long, have faced criticism from others for doing so. What these women are doing is the very definition of *jihad*. Far from the gross caricaturisation of 'war against the unbelievers', as it is so lazily mis-defined, *jihad* is struggle or exertion of effort, to change oneself and society for the better, and to stand up against oppression. The Muslim women I spoke with, and so many before and around them, were and are engaged in an important daily *jihad*—the struggle against sexism. This is the *jihad* that is far too infrequently documented, and we are all the poorer for our ignorance. When sexism destroys and limits, this responsive *jihad* builds, heals and protects. These women, and this *jihad*, is changing the world.

ACKNOWLEDGEMENTS

First thanks must go to the women I interviewed. Your generosity of time, wisdom and spirit was the delightful, unexpected joy of this research for me. I gained so much, personally and professionally, and this work literally could not exist without you. Recording your stories has been a privilege. *Jazakum Allahu khairan.*

This book is the unruly child of a more uptight PhD thesis parent. And so once again I must thank the greatest doctoral supervisors on the planet, Andrew Singleton and Pete Lentini, for being the guiding lights of this project's first incarnation. I would not have wanted to do this with any other supervisors. I owe you both more than I can ever say, and I aim to at least be half the academic—and feminist—you both are.

To the relentlessly uncomplaining and remarkable Sally Heath of MUP, who helped me sculpt the work from stuffy dissertation to more accessible book, ensuring the words of the women reached a far wider audience than my two doctoral examiners: thank you for being the loveliest publisher on the planet, and for not shredding my contract for testing your patience again and again and again. Immense thanks also to Scott Stephens, who arrived in a boat of hope when I was drowning with this work—you are the epitome of a good friend and a remarkable man of God.

Thank you to my colleagues at the National Centre for Australian Studies at Monash University for their support and collegiality, in particular Professor Bruce Scates for his eternal encouragement, wisdom and hilarity.

To my Mum, thank you for being my first example of a feminist and a woman. I love you incalculably. To Dad, Tanty and

Jan, thank you for being the wonderful parental figures you all are, and helping to create a family environment that always feels like a reassuring hug. Saara, Hena and Aneesa, calling you three my closest friends is an honour I hope extends beyond time. To Zayd, Aisha and Waleed, you are the best part of everything, and forever my 3BT.

Wa Allahu 'alim.

GLOSSARY

adhan	call to prayer (melodious)
daleel	evidence
daraba	key word in the controversial verse of 4:34 in the Qur'an; most often translated as 'beat', but has multiple other valid and commonly used translations
deen	religion, way of life
fatwa	(pl. *fatwas/fatawa*) non-binding religious edict only to be issued by people with adequate religious training
fitna	traditionally understood to mean 'civil discord' or 'civil strife', has taken on a sexualised undertone in modern times, and thus women can be accused of causing *fitna* simply by being women
hadith	(pl. *ahadith*) literally, report, account or statement. In Islamic law, 'a prophetic tradition transmitted through a chain of narrators by which the Prophet or his [way, practice] is known' (Abou El Fadl, 2001: 300)
hafiza	(feminine; *hafiz*, masculine) title given to someone who has memorised the entire Qur'an
haram	forbidden

hijab	term generally used to refer to the headscarf that still allows face and eyes to be seen and worn by some Muslim women
hijra	migration; commonly refers to the migration of the Prophet Muhammad and early Muslims from persecution in Mecca to safety in Medina
hudud	literally, 'limits'; specifically prescribed punishments in Islamic criminal law; i.e., cutting off the hand as punishment for theft
inshaAllah	God willing
jihad	to struggle or exert oneself for a godly cause
jummah	Friday congregational prayer
madhahib	(pl.; sing. *madhab*) schools of thought in Islamic jurisprudence
mahr	money that must be paid to a woman by her future husband upon marriage for her personal use, as a matter of religious obligation. Amount is un-set (the bride is the only one who can decide what it will be) and is often understood to be the woman's 'insurance' money for fiscal independence should the marriage end in either divorce or the death of her husband. It is also hers to spend as she sees fit even if she does not divorce or become a widow
mashaAllah	literally, 'This is what Allah wills'; often said to express surprise/joy
masjid	place of worship; also known as a 'mosque'
Muslimah	feminine version of 'Muslim'

nushuz	a highly contested and much-debated term, but generally understood to mean 'rebellion', 'disobedience', 'deliberate ill-conduct based on ill-will', 'gross misconduct', 'disloyalty', etc.
qadi	judge (title)
Quraysh	main tribe of Mecca at the time of the Prophet Muhammad
Qur'an	Holy book for Muslims; believed by Muslims to be the literal and unchanged word of God given to the Prophet Muhammad
RasooluLah	messenger of God; title or another way to refer to the Prophet Muhammad
salAllahu alayhi wasalam	literally, 'peace and blessings of Allah be upon him'; said whenever mentioning the Prophet Muhammad as a sign of respect
shariah	divine religious law
Shaykh	(masculine; feminine, *shaykha*) literally 'person with grey hair' but generally used to connote a learned, religious leader
Shirk	associating other partners with God—the greatest, and only unforgivable, sin in Islam
shurah	consultation, or consultative board; i.e., *shurah* board, *shurah* council; 'I will make *shurah* with that person', meaning, 'I will consult with that person'
sunnah	literally, 'way'; understood widely to be referring to the methodology of the Prophet Muhammad in all things he did. The *sunnah* is something practising Muslims want to emulate and hold up as the golden standard

tafsir	explanation, interpretation or commentary, particularly of the Qur'an
tajwid	melodious, traditional way of reciting Qur'an
tawhid	monotheism; the most important theological concept in Islam
ummah	global Muslim community
zina	adultery or pre-marital sex; a punishable offence in Islamic law—in Pakistan, rape falls under *zina* laws
zulm/dhulm	oppression

NOTES AND SOURCES

Dangerous Waters
Sources
Acker, S. (2000), 'In/out/side'
Leatherby, G. (2003), *Feminist Research in Theory and Practice*
Maguire, D.C. (2007), 'The religiously induced illness of women's subordination and its cure', in Daniel Maguire and Sa'diyya Shaikh (eds), *Violence against Women in Contemporary World Religion: Roots and Cures*, Cleveland: Pilgrim Press.
Zine, J. (2004), 'Creating a Critical Faith-Centered Space for Antiracist Feminism'

Chapter 1—Beyond the Harem
Notes
1. It is beyond the scope of this book to provide a full overview of this matter, but it is imperative to note that using terms such as 'The West' in absolutist ways is highly problematic and contested, especially when directly contrasted with the absolutist term 'Islam'—that is, 'Islam vs The West', for example. Said (2001) covers this topic in more detail. For the sake of brevity, I use terms such as 'The West' or 'The Western view', though it should be stressed that I do not do so in a 'clash of civilisations' Huntingtonian, absolutist way, or ignorant of the problems with such terms. Generally, these terms are used only to demarcate a widely understood demographic region, or reference a documented belief commonly found within that region.
2. It is important to note that it is not unusual not to know the first name of Imam ash-Shafi'i's mother—it was commonplace then for men *and* women to be referred to only as 'The mother/father of X' or 'The son/daughter of Y', as opposed to by their first name. There are male companions of the Prophet who, to this day, are known only as 'Abu X'

(Father of X), with no certainty of their first names. This was actually a sign of familial respect and honour, in much the same way adults in Western cultures used to be known solely as Mr or Mrs X, and no sexist reading should be inferred.

3   AH refers to 'After Hijra' and is the standard delineation of time used by Muslims instead of the 'BC: Before Christ'/'AD: Anno Domini' nomenclature used in Western/Christian societies. AH marks a time after the Prophet Muhammad and the early Muslims migrated (*hijra*) from Mecca to safety in Medina.
4   For further discussion on the complexities and contradictions within this issue, see Scott 1994.
5   Of course, many Iranian women were happy to unveil as well.

Sources

Abdalati, H. (1999), *Islam in Focus*
Abou El Fadl, K. (2001), *Speaking in God's Name*
—(2006), *A Conference of the Books*, p. 226
Abu-Lughod, L. (ed.) (1998), *Remaking Women*, p. 4
Adams, C.C. (1933), *Islam and Modernism*
Al-Hibri, A. (2000), 'An Introduction to Muslim Women's Rights'
Allen, C. (2010), *Islamophobia*
Alloula. M. (1986), *The Colonial Harem*
Badran, M. (2009), *Feminism in Islam*, pp. 223, 243, 244, 307
Barlas, A. (2005) 'Globalizing Equality', p. 91
BBC (2012), 'Nigerians Living in Poverty Rise to Nearly 61%'
Benn, T. & Jawad, H.A. (2003), Muslim Women in the United Kingdom and Beyond
Bonn, S. (2010), *Mass Deception*
Bunting, A. (2011), '"Authentic Sharia" as Cause and Cure for Women's Human Rights Violations in Northern Nigeria', pp. 162, 165
Bunting, M. (2011), 'What went wrong for Afghanistan's women?'
Chakrabarti, R. (2001), 'Cherie "lifts veil" for Afghan women'
Clarence-Smith, W.G. (2012), 'Female Circumcision in Southeast Asia since the Coming of Islam'
Fazaeli, R. (2012), 'Contemporary Iranian Feminisms'
Glick, P. & Fiske, S.T. (2001), 'An Ambivalent Alliance', p. 109
Hamdan, A. (2012), 'The Role of Authentic Islam'
Heffernan, V. (2009), 'Saving the World's Women'

Husseini, R. (2009), *Murder in the Name of Honour*
Kahf, M. (1999), *Western Representations of the Muslim Woman*
Kristof, N.D. & WuDunn, S. (2009), *Half the Sky*, p. 154
Lang, J. (1994), *Struggling to Surrender*
Lewis, R. & Micklewright, N. (eds) (2006), *Gender, Modernity and Liberty*, p. 1
Mahmood, S. (2005), *Politics of Piety*, pp. 1–2
Maumoon, D. (1999), 'Islamism and Gender Activism, pp. 275, 278
Mernissi, F. (1996), *Women's Rebellion and Islamic Memory*
Misciagno, P.S. (1997). *Rethinking Feminist Identification*, p. ix
Mogahed, D. & Esposito, J. (2007), *Who Speaks for Islam?*, p. 99
Moghissi, H. (1998), 'Women, Modernity, and Political Islam', quoting Nateq, 1358 AH/1980, p. 128
Morey, P. & Yaqin, A. (2010), 'Muslims in the Frame'
Morgan, G. & Poynting, S. (2012), *Global Islamophobia*, p. 15
Nadwi, M.A. (2007), *Al-Muhaddithat*, pp. xiv, 282
Nageeb, S.A. (2008), 'Diversified Development, p. 225
Poynting, et al. (2004), *Bin Laden in the Suburbs*
Roald, A.S. (1998), 'Feminist Reinterpretation of Islamic Sources', p. 20
Runnymede Trust (1997), *Islamophobia*, p. 1
Scott, J. (1994), 'Deconstructing Equality-versus-Difference'
Shaikh, S. (2003), 'Transforming Feminism'
Swindle, D. (2010), 'Feminist Hawk Rising!'
Van Sommer, A. & Zwemer, S.M. (1907), *Our Moslem Sisters*, p. 16
Wadud, A. (2006), *Inside the Gender Jihad*, pp. 4–5, 79
Yegenoglu, M. (1998), *Colonial Fantasies*
Zahedi, A. (2007), 'Contested Meaning of the Veil and Political Ideologies of Iranian Regimes'

Chapter 2—Witnesses to their Faith

Notes

1. For more on the diversity that exists among Muslim communities in Western countries, and the role of attachment to the global ummah within them, see Saeed and Akbarzadeh (2001), Bouma, et al. (2001), Singleton (2014).
2. For example, the book-banning case in Malaysia, where an academic compilation entitled *Muslim Women and the Challenges of Extremism* was banned (later over-turned in the High Court) because the Islamic

Development Department of Malaysia argued it 'could confuse Muslims, especially those with only a superficial knowledge of their religion'. See Magasawari (2010); see also Sikand (2010) who interviewed Mir-Hosseini, who said that for women in certain Arab countries to publicly argue for women's rights in the same way that Muslim women do in the West, Indonesia and Iran, for example, 'could well cost you your life. You could easily be branded as an apostate and killed'.

Sources

Australian Bureau of Statistics (2012), Reflecting a Nation
Badran, M. (2009), *Feminism in Islam*, pp. 1, 235
Baktiar, L. (2007), *The Sublime Quran*
Barlas, A. (2002), *'Believing Women'*
Bouma G., et al. (2001), 'Muslims Managing Religious Diversity'
DeVault, M.L. (1996), 'Talking Back to Sociology'
Finch, J. (1993), 'It's Great Having Someone to Talk to'
Magaswari, M. (2010), 'Ban Lifted on Sisters in Islam Book'
Mattu, A. & Maznavi, N. (2012), *Love, InshaAllah*
Nomani, A. (2006), *Standing Alone*, pp. viii–xiv
Pew Forum (2011), Pew Research Center's Forum on Religion and Public Life, p. 77
Quraishi-Landes, A. (1997), 'Her Honor'
— (2011), 'What if Sharia Weren't the Enemy'
Ramadan, T. (2004), *Western Muslims and the Future of Islam*, p. 4
Saeed, A. & Akbarzadeh, S. (eds) (2001), *Muslim Communities in Australia*
Sikand, Y. (2010), 'Understanding Islamic Feminism'
Singleton, A. (2014), *Religion, Culture and Society*
Wadud, A. (1993) *Qur'an and Woman*
— (2006), *Inside the Gender Jihad*, p. 262
Webb, G. (ed.) (2000), *Windows of Faith*

Chapter 3—Journey to the Fight

Sources

Barazangi, N.H. (2004), *Woman's Identity and the Qur'an*, p. 22
Cowan, G., et al. (1992), 'Predictors of Feminist Self-labelling'
Haddad, Y. (2005), 'The Study of Women in Islam and the West', pp. 113, 114

Jouili, J.S. & Amir-Moazami, S. (2006), 'Knowledge, Empowerment and Religious Authority Among Pious Muslim Women in France and Germany'
Korman, S. (1983), 'The Feminist-familial Influences on Adherence to Ideology and Commitment to a Self-perception'
Maguire, D.C. (2007), 'Introduction: The religiously induced illness of women's subordination and its cure', p. 1
Schüssler Fiorenza, E. (1984), *Bread not Stones*, p. 138
Shaikh, S. (2004), 'Knowledge, Women and Gender in *Hadith*, p. 99
Wadud, A. (2006), *Inside the Gender Jihad*, p. 5

Chapter 4—Encouragement, Hostility, Apathy

Note

1 Started in 1930 in Detroit, the Nation of Islam is a religio-political group that advocates for the separation of black and white Americans. It has been accused of being a black supremacist group and a hate group, and is also accused of having core teachings that contravene orthodox Islamic norms.

Sources

Alexander, S. & Ryan, M. (1997), 'Social Constructs of Feminism'
al-Khayyat, S. (1990), *Honour and Shame*, p. 23
Aly, W. (2007), *People Like Us*, pp. 51–52
Buschman, J.K. & Lenart, S. (1996), 'I'm Not a Feminist, but …'
Callaghan, M., et al. (1999), 'Feminism in Scotland'
Goldberg, P.A., et al. (1975), 'Another Put-down of Women?'
Harris, C. (2004), *Control and Subversion*
Hassan, M. (2012), 'Reshaping Religious Authority in Contemporary Turkey'
Jamieson, K.H. (1995), *Beyond the Double Bind*
Mansbridge, J. (1986), *Why We Lost the E.R.A.*
Manville, J. (1997), 'The Gendered Organization of an Australian Anglican Parish', p. 37
Nnaemeka, O. (2004), 'Nego-feminism, pp. 377–78, 380
Rouse, C.M. (2004), *Engaged Surrender*, p. 31
Rudman, L. & Fairchild, K. (2007), 'The F Word'

Steuter, E. (1992), 'Women Against Feminism'
Twenge, J.M. & Zucker, A.N. (2006), 'What is a Feminist?'

Chapter 5—The Double Bind
Note
1. It is important to note that, far from being passive non-responders, there has been significant, diverse and robust mainstream media engagement by Muslims, including Muslim women, in the communities I researched. See Lentini, Dreher, Carland.

Sources
Beale, F. (1979), 'Double Jeopardy'
Carland, S. (2012), 'Silenced'
Dreher, T. (2010), 'Community Media Intervention', pp. 201, 202
Hidayatullah A. (2014), *Feminist Edges of the Qur'an*, p. ix
Ho, C. (2007), 'Muslim Women's New Defenders', p. 296
hooks, b. (1984), *Feminist Theory*, p. 118
— (1994), *Outlaw Culture*, pp. 116, 118, 123
Human Rights and Equal Opportunity Commission (2003), 'Isma Listen'
Hussein, S. (2010), 'Double Bind and Double Responsibility', p. 159
Khan, S. (2013), 'Muslim Women are Caught in the Crossfire Between Bigots on Both Sides'
King, D. (1988), 'Multiple Jeopardy, Multiple Consciousness'
Lentini, P. (2008), 'Muslim Media Interventions'
Morey, P. & Yaqin, A. (2010), 'Muslims in the Frame', p. 153
Persad, J.V. & Lukas, S. (2002), 'No Hijab Permitted Here'
Rose, T. (1990), 'Never Trust a Big Butt and a Smile', p. 113

Chapter 6—The Third Way: Faith and Feminism
Sources
Al-Hibri, A. (1997), 'Islam, Law and Custom', p. 3
Ali, K. (2006), *Sexual Ethics and Islam*, p. xii
Ali, S.R., et al. (2008), 'A Qualitative Investigation of Muslim and Christian Women's Views of Religion and Feminism in their Lives', pp. 38–39, 43, 45, 46
An-Na'im, A.A. (1996), *Toward an Islamic Reformation*, p. 11

Badran, M. (2009), *Feminism in Islam*, pp. 218, 219, 243, 245, 246
Barazangi, N.H. (2004), 'Understanding Muslim Women's Self-identity and Resistance to Feminism and Participatory Action Research', p. 22
Barlas, A. (2005) 'Globalizing Equality', p. 97
Gillis, S., et al. (2007), *Third Wave Feminism*, p. xxiv
Groenhout, R.E. & Bower, M. (eds) (2003), *Philosophy, Feminism and Faith*
Gross, R.M. (1996), *Feminism and Religion*
Heywood, L.L. (ed.) (2006), *The Women's Movement Today*, p. xx
Jayawardena, K. (1986), *Feminism and Nationalism in the Third World*
Moghissi, H. (1998), 'Women, Modernity, and Political Islam', quoting Nateq, 1358 AH/1980
Quraishi-Landes, A. (2011), 'What if Sharia Weren't the Enemy', p. 176
Russell, L. (ed.) (1985), *Feminist Interpretation of the Bible*
Sandoval, C. (1991), 'US Third World Feminism', p. 4
Sharma, A. & Young, K. (eds) (1999), *Feminism and World Religions*
Singleton, A. (2014), *Religion, Culture and Society*, p. 188
Treacher, A. (2003), 'Reading the Other', p. 65

BIBLIOGRAPHY

ABC News (2009), 'Call for hijab ban sparks community outrage' 2009, www.abc.net.au/news/2009-01-15/call-for-hijab-ban-sparks-community-outrage/268182.

Abdalati, H. (1999), *Islam in Focus*, Rahmah Publishers, India.

Abou El Fadl, K. (2001), *Speaking in God's Name: Islamic law, authority and women*, Oneworld, Virginia.

— (2006), *A Conference of the Books: A search for beauty in Islam*, Rowman and Littlefield Publishers Inc., USA.

Abu-Lughod, L. (1986), *Veiled Sentiments: Honor and poetry in a Bedouin society*, University of California Press, USA.

— (ed.) (1998), *Remaking Women: Feminism and modernity in the Middle East*, Princeton University Press, New Jersey.

Acker, S. (2000), 'In/out/side: Positioning the researcher in feminist qualitative research', *Resources for Feminist Research*, no. 28, pp. 1–2.

Adams, C.C. (1933), *Islam and Modernism: A study of the modern reform movement inaugurated by Muhammad 'Abduh*, The American University, Cairo.

Adell, S. (1994), *Double Consciousness/Double Bind*, University of Illinois Press, Illinois.

Adelman, M., Erez, E. & Shalhoub-Kevorkian, N. (2003), 'Policing Violence Against Minority Women in Multicultural Societies: "Community" and the politics of exclusion', *Police and Society*, vol. 7, pp. 103–31.

Ahmed, L. (1992), *Women and Gender in Islam: Historical roots of a modern debate*, Yale University Press, Michigan.

Al-Hibri, A. (1997), 'Islam, Law and Custom: Redefining Muslim women's rights', *American University Journal of International Law and Policy*, vol. 12, pp. 1–44.

— (2000), 'An Introduction to Muslim Women's Rights' in Gisela Webb (ed.), *Windows of Faith: Muslim women scholar–activists in North America*, Syracuse University Press, New York.

al-Khayyat, S. (1990), *Honour and Shame: Women in modern Iraq*, Saqi Books, Wiltshire.
Alexander, S. & Ryan, M. (1997), 'Social Constructs of Feminism: A study of undergraduates at a women's college', *College Student Journal*, vol. 31, pp. 555–67.
Ali, K. (2006), *Sexual Ethics and Islam: Feminist reflections on Qur'an, hadith, and jurisprudence*, OneWorld Publishing, Oxford.
Ali, S.R., Mahmood, A., Moel, J., Hudson, C. & Leathers, L. (2008), 'A Qualitative Investigation of Muslim and Christian Women's Views of Religion and Feminism in their Lives', *Cultural Diversity and Ethnic Minority Psychology*, vol. 14, no. 1, pp. 38–46.
Allen, C. (2010), *Islamophobia*, Ashgate Publishing, Surrey.
Alloula, M. (1986), *The Colonial Harem*, Manchester University Press, Glasgow.
Aly, W. (2007), *People Like Us: How arrogance is dividing Islam and the West*, Picador, Sydney.
An-Na'im, A.A. (1996), *Toward an Islamic Reformation: Civil liberties, human rights, and international law*, Syracuse University Press, New York.
Anderson, K.J., Kanner, M. & Elsayegh, N. (2009), 'Are Feminists Man Haters? Feminists' and nonfeminists' attitudes toward men', *Psychology of Women Quarterly*, vol. 33, no. 2, pp. 216–24.
Aronson, P. (2003), 'Feminists or "Postfeminists"? Young women's attitudes toward feminism and gender relations', *Gender and Society*, vol. 17, pp. 903–22.
Australian Bureau of Statistics (2012), Reflecting a Nation: Stories from the 2011 census, 2012–2013, ABS, Canberra, cat no. 2071.0.
Badawy, M. (2007), 'Woman Re-interprets Koran with Feminist View', *Reuters*, 22 March, www.reuters.com/article/ 2007/03/23/us-koran-feminist-id USN2129015920070323.
Badran, M. (1995), *Feminists, Islam, and Nation: Gender and the making of modern Egypt*, Princeton University Press, West Sussex.
— (2009), *Feminism in Islam: Secular and religious convergences*, One World, Oxford.
Baktiar, L. (2007), *The Sublime Quran*, Islamicworld.com, Chicago.
Barazangi, N.H. (2004), 'Understanding Muslim Women's Self-identity and Resistance to Feminism and Participatory Action Research' in Brydon-Miller, M., Maguire, P. & McIntyre, A. (eds), *Traveling Companions: Feminism, teaching and action research*, Praeger, Conneticut.

— (2004), *Woman's Identity and the Qur'an: A new reading*, University Press of Florida, Florida.

Barlas, A. (2002), 'Believing Women' in *Islam: Unreading patriarchal interpretations of the Quran*, University of Texas Press, Austin.

— (2005) 'Globalizing Equality: Muslim women, theology and feminism' in Fereshteh Nouraie-Simone (ed.), *On Shifting Ground: Muslim women in the global era*, The Feminist Press, New York.

BBC (2012), 'Nigerians Living in Poverty Rise to Nearly 61%', *BBC News Africa*, 13 February, www.bbc.com/news/world-africa-17015873.

Beale, F. (1979), 'Double Jeopardy: to be black and female' in Toni Cade (ed.), *The Black Woman: An anthology*, New American Library, New York.

Beasley, C. (1999), *What is Feminism? An introduction to feminist theory*, Sage, Australia.

Benn, T. & Jawad, H.A. (2003), *Muslim Women in the United Kingdom and Beyond: Experiences and images*, Sage, London.

Bhavnani, K.K. & Davis, A.Y. (1989), 'Complexity, Activism, Optimism: An interview with Angela Y. Davis', *Feminist Review*, vol. 31, pp. 66–81.

Bonn, S. (2010), *Mass Deception: Moral panic and the US War on Iraq*, Rutgers University Press, New Jersey.

Bouma, G. (2001), *The Research Process* (4th edition), Oxford University Press, South Melbourne.

Bouma, G., Daw, J. & Munawwar, R. (2001), 'Muslims Managing Religious Diversity' in Abdullah Saeed and Shahram Akbarzadeh (eds), *Muslim Communities in Australia*, UNSW Press, Sydney.

Brooks, A. & Hesse-Biber, S.N. (2007), 'An Invitation to Feminist Research' in Sharlene Nagy Hesse-Biber & Patricia Lina Leavy (eds), *Feminist Research Practice: A primer*, Sage, Thousand Oaks.

Bunting, A. (2011), '"Authentic Sharia" as Cause and Cure for Women's Human Rights Violations in Northern Nigeria', *Journal of Women of the Middle East and the Islamic World*, vol. 9, pp. 152–70.

Bunting, M. (2011), 'What went wrong for Afghanistan's women?' *The Guardian*, 26 September, www.theguardian.com/global-development/poverty-matters/2011/sep/26/afghanistan-women-what-went-wrong.

Buschman, J.K. & Lenart, S. (1996), '"I'm Not a Feminist, but …": College women, feminism, and negative experiences, *Political Psychology*, vol. 17, pp. 59–75.

Bush, L. (2001), 'Text: Laura Bush on Taliban oppression of women', *The Washington Post*, 17 November 2001, www.washingtonpost.com/wp-srv/nation/specials/attacked/transcripts/laurabushtext_111701.html.

Callaghan, M., Cranmer, C., Rowan, M., Siann, G., & Wilson, F. (1999), 'Feminism in Scotland: Self-identification and stereotypes', *Gender and Education*, vol. 11, no. 2, pp. 161–78.

Carland, S. (2012), 'Silenced: Muslim women commentators in the Australian media', *The La Trobe Journal*, no. 89, pp. 140+.

Chakrabarti, R. (2001), 'Cherie "lifts veil" for Afghan women', *BBC News*, 19 November 2001, news.bbc.co.uk/2/hi/uk_news/politics/1665017.stm.

Chow, E.N-L. (1987), 'The Development of Feminist Consciousness Among Asian-American Women', *Gender & Society*, vol. 1, no. 3.

Clarence-Smith, W.G. (2012), 'Female Circumcision in Southeast Asia since the Coming of Islam' in Chitra Raghavan and James P. Levine (eds), *Self-determination and Women's Rights in Muslim Societies*, Brandeis University Press, Massachusetts.

Cowan, G., Mestlin, M. & Masek, J. (1992), 'Predictors of Feminist Self-labelling', *Sex Roles*, vol. 27, no. 7–8, pp. 321–30.

Darwish, N. (2006), *Now They Call Me Infidel: Why I renounced jihad for America, Israel, and the War on Terror*, Sentinel, New York.

DeVault, M.L. (1996), 'Talking Back to Sociology: Distinctive contributions of feminist methodology', *Annual Review of Sociology*, vol. 22, pp. 29–50.

Doorn-Harder, (2012). 'Translating Text to Context: Muslim women activists in Indonesia' in Masooda Bano and Hilary Kalmbach (eds), *Women, Leadership, and Mosques: Changes in contemporary Islamic authority*, Brill, The Netherlands.

Dreher, T. (2010), 'Community Media Intervention' in M. Abdalla, J. Ewart & H. Rane (eds), *Islam and the Australian News Media*, Melbourne University Press, Melbourne.

Eid, A. (dir) (2014), *UnMosqued*, DVD, USA.

Fadel, M. (1997), 'Two Women, One Man: Knowledge, power and gender in medieval Sunni legal thought', *International Journal of Middle Eastern Studies*, vol. 29, pp. 185–204.

Farquharson, K. (2005), 'A Different Kind of Snowball: Identifying key policymakers', *International Journal of Social Research Methodology*, vol. 8, no. 4, pp. 345–53.

Fazaeli, R. (2012), 'Contemporary Iranian Feminisms: Definitions, narratives and identity' in Chitra Raghavan, James P. Levine (eds),

Self-determination and Women's Rights in Muslim Societies, Brandeis University Press, Massachusetts.

Fernea, E.W. (1998), *In Search of Islamic Feminism: One woman's global journey*, Anchor books, New York.

Finch, J. (1993), '"It's Great Having Someone to Talk to": Ethics and politics of interviewing women' in Martyn Hammersley (ed.), *Social Research: Philosophy, politics and practice*, Sage Publications, London.

Foucault, M. (1980), *Power/Knowledge*, Pantheon, New York.

Gay, C. and Tate, K. (1998), 'Doubly Bound: The impact of gender and race on the politics of black women', *Political Psychology*, vol. 19, no. 1, pp. 169–84.

Gillis, S., Howie, G. & Munford, R. (2007), *Third Wave Feminism: A critical exploration* (expanded second edition), Palgrave Macmillan, New York.

Glick, P. & Fiske, S.T. (1996), 'The Ambivalent Sexism Inventory: Differentiating hostile and benevolent sexism', *Journal of Personality and Social Psychology*, vol. 70, pp. 491–512.

— (2001), 'An Ambivalent Alliance: Hostile and benevolent sexism as complementary justifications for gender inequality', *American Psychologist*, vol. 56, no. 2, pp. 109–18.

Gluck, S.B. & Patai, D. (eds) (1991), *Women's Words: The feminist practice of oral history*, Routledge, New York.

Goldberg, P.A., Gottesdiener, M., & Abramson, P.R. (1975), 'Another Putdown of Women? Perceived attractiveness as a function of support for the feminist movement', *Journal of Personality and Social Psychology*, vol. 32, no. 1, pp. 113–15.

Gottshalk, P. & Greenberg, G. (2008), *Islamophobia: Making Muslims the enemy*, Rowman and Littlefield Publishers, Plymouth.

Groenhout, R.E. & Bower, M. (eds) (2003), *Philosophy, Feminism and Faith*, University Press Indiana, Indiana.

Gross, R.M. (1996), *Feminism and Religion: An introduction*, Beacon Press, Massachusetts.

Guardi, J. (2004), 'Women Reading the Qur'an: Religious discourse and Islam', *Hawwa*, vol. 2, no. 3, pp. 301–15.

Haddad, Y. (2005), 'The Study of Women in Islam and the West: A select bibliography', *Hawwa*, vol. 3, no. 1, pp. 111–57.

Hamdan, A. (2012), 'The Role of Authentic Islam: The way forward for women in Saudi Arabia', *Journal of Women of the Middle East and the Islamic World*, vol. 10, pp. 200–20.

Hammer, J. (2012), 'Activism As Embodied Tafsir: Negotiating women's authority, leadership, and space in North America' in Masooda Bano and Hilary Kalmbach (eds), *Women, Leadership, and Mosques: Changes in Contemporary Islamic Authority*, Brill, The Netherlands.

Harding, S. (1986), 'Is There a Feminist Method?' in Sandra Kemp and Judith Squires (eds), Feminisms, Oxford University Press, Oxford.

Harris, C. (2004), *Control and Subversion: Gender relations in Tajikistan*, Pluto Press, USA.

Hashim, I. (1999), 'Reconciling Islam and Feminism', *Gender and Development*, vol. 7, no. 1, pp. 7–14.

Hassan, M. (2012), 'Reshaping Religious Authority in Contemporary Turkey: State-sponsored female preachers', in Masooda Bano and Hilary Kalmbach (eds), *Women, Leadership, and Mosques: Changes in contemporary Islamic authority*, Brill, The Netherlands.

Heffernan, V. (2009), 'Saving the World's Women: The feminism hawks', *The New York Times*, 19 August, www.nytimes.com/2009/08/23/magazine/23FOB-medium-t.html?_r=0.

Heywood, L.L. (ed.) (2006), *The Women's Movement Today: An Encyclopedia of Third-Wave Feminism*, vol. 1, A–Z, Greenwood, Westport, CT.

Hidayatullah, A. (2014), *Feminist Edges of the Qur'an*, Oxford University Press, New York.

Hirsi Ali, A. (2006), *The Caged Virgin: An emancipation proclamation for women and Islam*, Simon and Schuster, New York.

— (2007), *Infidel*, Atria Paperback, New York.

— (2010), *Nomad: From Islam to America: A personal journey through the clash of civilizations*, Free Press, New York.

Ho, C. (2007), 'Muslim Women's New Defenders: Women's rights, nationalism and Islamophobia in contemporary Australia', *Women's Studies International Forum*, vol. 30, pp. 290–98.

hooks, b. (1984), *Feminist Theory: From margin to centre*, South End Press, Boston.

— (1994), *Outlaw Culture: Resisting representations*, Routlege, New York.

Houston, M. & Kramarae, C. (1991), 'Speaking from Silence: Methods of silencing and of resistance', *Discourse and Society*, vol. 2, no. 4, pp. 387–99.

Human Rights and Equal Opportunity Commission (2003), 'Isma Listen: National consultations on eliminating prejudice against Arab and Muslim Australians', Melbourne.

Hussein, S. (2010), 'Double Bind and Double Responsibility: Speech and silence among Australian Muslim women' in Shahram Akbarzadeh (ed.), *Challenging Identities: Muslim women in Australia*, Melbourne University Press, Carlton.

Husseini, R. (2009), *Murder in the Name of Honour*, OneWorld Publications, England.

Islam, S. (2012), 'The Qubaysīyyāt: The growth of an international Muslim women's revivalist movement from Syria (1960–2008)' in Masooda Bano and Hilary Kalmbach (eds), *Women, Leadership, and Mosques: Changes in contemporary Islamic authority*, Brill, The Netherlands.

James, J. (ed.) (1998), *The Angela Y. Davis Reader*, Wiley-Blackwell, Cornwall.

Jamieson, K.H. (1995), *Beyond the Double Bind: Women and leadership*, Oxford University Press, New York.

Jaschok, M. (2012), 'Sources of Authority: Female ahong and Qingzhen Nüsi (women's mosques) in China' in Masooda Bano and Hilary Kalmbach (eds), *Women, Leadership, and Mosques: Changes in Contemporary Islamic Authority*, Brill, The Netherlands.

Jawad, H. (2009), 'Islamic Feminism: Leadership roles and public representation', *Hawwa*, vol. 7, no. 1, pp. 1–24.

Jaworska, S. & Krishnamurthy, R. (2012), 'On the F Word: A corpus-based analysis of the media representation of feminism in British and German press discourse, 1990–2009', *Discourse and Society*, vol. 23, no. 4, pp. 401–31.

Jayawardena, K. (1986), *Feminism and Nationalism in the Third World*, Zed Books Ltd, London.

Jeffery, P., Jeffery, R. & Jeffrey, C. (2012), 'Leading by Example? Women madrasah teachers in rural North India' in Masooda Bano and Hilary Kalmbach (eds), *Women, Leadership, and Mosques: Changes in contemporary Islamic authority*, Brill, The Netherlands.

Johnson, B. (2007), 'What Islamic terrorists are really afraid of is women', *The Telegraph*, 27 September.

Jonker, G. (2003), 'Islamic Knowledge Through a Woman's Lens: Education, power and belief', *Social Compass*, vol. 50, no. 1, pp. 35–46.

Jouili, J.S. & Amir-Moazami, S. (2006), 'Knowledge, Empowerment and Religious Authority Among Pious Muslim Women in France and Germany', *The Muslim World*, vol. 96, no. 4, pp. 617–42.

Kahf, M. (1999), *Western Representations of the Muslim Woman: From termagant to odalisque*, University of Texas Press, Austin.

Kandiyoti, D. (1988), 'Bargaining with Patriarchy', *Gender and Society*, vol. 2, no. 3, pp. 274–90.

Khan, S. (2013), 'Muslim Women are Caught in the Crossfire Between Bigots on Both Sides', *The Guardian*, 11 March.

King, D. (1988), 'Multiple Jeopardy, Multiple Consciousness: The context of a black feminist ideology', *Signs: Journal of Women in Culture and Society*, vol. 14, no. 1, pp. 42–72.

Korman, S. (1983), 'The Feminist-familial Influences on Adherence to Ideology and Commitment to a Self-perception', *Family Relations*, vol. 39, pp. 431–39.

Kristof, N.D. & WuDunn, S. (2009), *Half the Sky*, Alfred A. Knopf, USA.

Lang, J. (1994), *Struggling to Surrender: Some impressions of an American convert to Islam*, Amana Publications, Maryland.

Le Renard, A. (2012), 'From Qur'anic Circles to the Internet: Gender segregation and the rise of female preachers in Saudi Arabia' in Masooda Bano and Hilary Kalmbach (eds), *Women, Leadership, and Mosques: Changes in contemporary Islamic authority*, Brill, The Netherlands.

Leatherby, G. (2003), *Feminist Research in Theory and Practice*, Open University Press, Philadelphia.

Lee, R.M. (1993), *Doing Research on Sensitive Topics*, Sage, California.

Lehmann, U.C. (2012), 'Women's Rights to Mosque Space: Access and participation in Cape Town mosques' in Masooda Bano and Hilary Kalmbach (eds), *Women, Leadership, and Mosques: Changes in contemporary Islamic authority*, Brill, The Netherlands.

Lentini, P. (2008), 'Muslim Media Interventions: Social capital, social cohesion and human security in the struggle against terrorism', Counter-Terrorism International Conference 2007, 15–16 October 2007, Victoria Police and Monash University, Australia, pp. 12–18.

Lewis, R. & Micklewright, N. (eds) (2006), *Gender, Modernity and Liberty: Middle Eastern women's writings—a critical sourcebook*, I.B. Tauris, Cornwall.

Lichter, I. (2009), *Muslim Women Reformers*, Prometheus Books, New York.

Lind, R.A. & Salo, C. (2006), 'The Framing of Feminists and Feminism in News and Public Affairs Programs in US Electronic Media', *Journal of Communication*, vol. 52, no. 1, pp. 211–28.

Loo, C. & Ong, P. (1982), 'Slaying Demons with a Sewing Needle: Feminist issues for Chinatown women', *Berkeley Journal of Sociology*, vol. 27, pp. 77–88.

Lu, L. (1982), 'Critical Visions: The representation and resistance of Asian women' in Sonia Shah (ed.), *Dragon Ladies: Asian American feminists breathe fire*, South End Press, Boston.

Magaswari, M. (2010), 'Ban Lifted on Sisters in Islam Book', *The Star*, 25 January, thestar.com.my/news/story.asp?file=/2010/1/25/nation/2010012515415 0&sec=nation.

Maguire, D.C. (2007), 'Introduction: The religiously induced illness of women's subordination and its cure' in Daniel Maguire and Sa'diyya Shaikh (eds), *Violence Against Women in Contemporary World Religion: Roots and cures*, Pilgrim Press, Cleveland.

Mahmood, S. (2005), *Politics of Piety: The Islamic revival and the feminist subject*, Princeton University Press, New Jersey.

Makki, H. (2015), 'Side Entrance', Tumblr, sideentrance.tumblr.com/.

Maltby, L.E., Hall, M.E.L., Anderson, T.L. & Edwards, K. (2010), 'Religion and Sexism: The moderating role of participant gender', *Sex Roles*, vol. 62, nos. 9–10, pp. 615–22.

Manji, I. (2003), *The Trouble with Islam Today: A Muslim's call for reform in her faith*, St Martin's Press, New York.

Mansbridge, J. (1986), *Why We Lost the E.R.A.*, University of Chicago Press, Chicago.

Manville, J. (1997), 'The Gendered Organization of an Australian Anglican Parish', *Sociology of Religion*, vol. 58, no. 1, pp. 25–38.

Massola, J. (2014), 'Burqa Crack Down: "Facial coverings" restricted in Parliament House public galleries', *The Sydney Morning Herald*, 2 October, www.smh.com.au/federal-politics/political-news/burqa-crackdown-facial-coverings-restricted-in-parliament-house-public-galleries-20141002-10p8pl.html.

Mattu, A. & Maznavi, N. (2012), *Love, InshaAllah: The secret love lives of Muslim American women*, Soft Skull Press, USA.

Maumoon, D. (1999), 'Islamism and Gender Activism: Muslim women's quest for autonomy', *Journal of Muslim Minority Affairs*, vol. 19, no. 2, pp. 269–83.

McCaffrey, D. (1998), 'Victim Feminism/Victim Activism', *Sociological Spectrum: Mid-south Sociological Association*, vol. 18, no. 3, pp. 263–84.

Mernissi, F. (1996), *Women's Rebellion and Islamic Memory*, Zed Books, USA.

Micinski, N.R. (2012), 'Celebrating Miss Muslim Pageants and Opposing Rock Concerts: Contrasting the religious authority and leadership of two Muslim women in Kazan' in Masooda Bano and Hilary Kalmbach (eds),

Women, Leadership, and Mosques: Changes in contemporary Islamic authority, Brill, The Netherlands.

Minganti, P.K. (2012), 'Challenging from Within: Youth associations and female leadership in Swedish mosques' in Masooda Bano and Hilary Kalmbach (eds), *Women, Leadership, and Mosques: Changes in contemporary Islamic authority*, Brill, The Netherlands.

Misciagno, P.S. (1997), *Rethinking Feminist Identification: The case for de facto feminism*, Praeger Publishers, Connecticut.

Mogahed, D. & Esposito, J. (2007), *Who Speaks for Islam?: What a billion Muslims really think*, Gallup Press, New York.

Moghissi, H. (1998), 'Women, Modernity, and Political Islam', *Iran Bulletin* (now *Middle East Left Forum*) nos. 19–20, pp. 42–44, quoting Nateq, 1358 AH/1980.

Morey, P. & Yaqin, A. (2010), 'Muslims in the Frame—introduction', *Interventions: International Journal of Postcolonial Studies*, vol. 12, no. 2, pp. 145–56.

Morgan, G. & Poynting, S. (2012), *Global Islamophobia: Muslims and Moral Panic in the West*, Farnham, Ashgate.

Nadwi, M.A. (2007), *Al-Muhaddithat: The women scholars in Islam*, Interface Publications, Istanbul.

Nageeb, S.A. (2008), 'Diversified Development: Women's agency and the constitution of translocal spaces' in Gudrun Lachenmann and Petra Dannecker (eds), *Negotiating Development in Muslim Societies: Gendered spaces and translocal connections*, Lexington Books, USA.

Nespor, J. (2000), 'Anonymity and Place in Social Inquiry', *Qualitative Inquiry*, vol. 6, no. 4, pp. 546–69.

Nnaemeka, O. (2004), 'Nego-feminism: Theorizing, practicing, and pruning Africa's way', *Signs*, vol. 29, no. 2, pp. 357–86.

Nomani, A. (2006), *Standing Alone: An American woman's struggle for the soul of Islam*, Harper Collins, USA.

Nouraie-Simone, F. (ed.) (2005), *On Shifting Ground: Muslim women in the global era*, The Feminist Press, New York.

Oakley, A. (1981), 'Interviewing Women: A contradiction in terms' in Yvonna S. Lincoln and Norman K. Denzin (eds), *Turning Points in Qualitative Research: Tying knots in a handkerchief*, AltaMira Press, California.

Owen, R. (2004), *Lord Cromer: Victorian imperialist, Edwardian proconsul*, Oxford University Press, Oxford.

Persad, J.V. & Lukas, S. (2002), '"No Hijab Permitted Here": A study on the experiences of Muslim women wearing hijab applying for work in the manufacturing, sales and service sectors', Women Working with Immigrant Women Report.

Pew Forum (2008), Pew Research Center's Forum on Religion and Public Life, *U.S. Religious Landscape Survey—Religious affiliation: Diverse and dynamic*, Pew Research Center, Washington DC.

— (2011), Pew Research Center's Forum on Religion and Public Life: The future of the global Muslim population: projections for 2010–2030, Pew Research Center, Washington DC.

Pierce, M. (2012), 'Remembering Fatimah: New means of legitimizing female authority in contemporary Shi'I discourse' in Masooda Bano and Hilary Kalmbach (eds), *Women, Leadership, and Mosques: Changes in contemporary Islamic authority*, Brill, The Netherlands.

Poynting, S., Noble, G., Tabar, P. & Collins, J. (2004), *Bin Laden in the Suburbs: Criminalising the Arab other*, Institute of Criminology, Sydney.

Putnam, R. (2000), *Bowling Alone: The collapse and revival of American community*, Simon and Schuster, New York.

Quraishi-Landes, A. (1997), 'Her Honor: An Islamic critique of the rape laws of Pakistan from a woman-sensitive perspective', *Michigan Journal of International Law*, vol. 18, pp. 287–320.

— (2011), 'What if Sharia Weren't the Enemy: Rethinking international women's rights advocacy on Islamic law', *Columbia Journal of Gender & Law*, vol. 22, pp. 173+.

Ramadan, T. (2004), *Western Muslims and the Future of Islam*, Oxford University Press, New York.

Ramazanoglu, C. & Holland, J. (2002), *Feminist Methodology: Challenges and choices*, Sage, Wiltshire.

Rausch, M.J. (2012), 'Women Mosque Preachers and Spiritual Guides: Publicizing and negotiating women's religious authority in Morocco' in Masooda Bano and Hilary Kalmbach (eds), *Women, Leadership, and Mosques: Changes in contemporary Islamic authority*, Brill, The Netherlands.

Reid, P.T. (1984), 'Feminism Versus Minority Group Identity: Not for black women only', *Sex Roles*, vol. 10, nos. 3/4, pp. 247–55.

Renzetti, C.M. (1987), 'New Wave or Second Stage? Attitudes of college women toward feminism', *Sex Roles*, vol. 16, pp. 265–77.

Rhode, D.L. (1995), 'Media Images, Feminist Issues', *Signs*, vol. 20, no. 3, pp. 685–710.

Roald, A.S. (1998), 'Feminist Reinterpretation of Islamic Sources: Muslim feminist theology in the light of the Christian tradition of feminist thought' in K. Ask and M. Tjomsland (eds), *Women and Islamization: Contemporary dimensions on discourse on gender relations*, Oxford, Berg.

Rose, T. (1990), 'Never Trust a Big Butt and a Smile', *Camera Obscura*, vol. 8, no. 2, pp. 108–31.

Rouse, C.M. (2004), *Engaged Surrender: African-American women and Islam*, University of California Press, London.

Rudman, L. & Fairchild, K. (2007), 'The F Word: Is feminism incompatible with beauty and romance?', *Psychology of Women Quarterly*, vol. 31, no. 2, pp. 125–36.

Runnymede Trust (1997), *Islamophobia: A challenge for us all*, The Runnymede Trust, England.

Russell, L. (ed.) (1985), *Feminist Interpretation of the Bible*, Westminster Press, Pennsylvania.

Saeed, A. & Akbarzadeh, S. (eds) (2001), *Muslim Communities in Australia*, UNSW Press, NSW.

Said, E. (2001), 'The Clash of Ignorance', *The Nation*, 22 October.

Sandoval, C. (1991), 'US Third World Feminism: The theory and method of oppositional consciousness in the postmodern world', *Genders*, vol. 10, pp. 1–24.

Sarup, M. (1988), *An Introductory Guide to Post-structuralism and Post Modernism*, Harvester Wheatsheaf, New York.

Schüssler Fiorenza, E. (1984), *Bread not Stones*, Beacon Press, Boston.

Scott, J. (1994), 'Deconstructing Equality-versus-Difference: Or, the uses of poststructuralist theory for feminism' in Joan W. Scott, *The Postmodern Turn: New perspectives on social theory*, pp. 15, 282+.

— (2013), *Social Network Analysis* (3rd edition), Sage, Cornwall.

Shah, P. (1982), 'Redefining the Home: How community elites silence feminist activism' in Sonia Shah (ed.), *Dragon Ladies: Asian American feminists breathe fire*, South End Press, Boston.

Shaikh, S. (2003), 'Transforming Feminism: Islam, women and gender justice' in Omid Safi (ed.), *Progressive Muslims on Justice, Gender and Pluralism*, OneWorld Publications, Oxford.

— (2004), 'Knowledge, Women and Gender in *Hadith*: A feminist interpretation', *Islam and Christian-Muslim Relations*, vol. 15, no. 1, pp. 99–108.

Sharify-Funk, M. (2008), *Encountering the Transnational: Women, Islam and the politics of interpretation*, Ashgate Publishing, Farnham.

Sharma, A. & Young, K. (eds) (1999), *Feminism and World Religions*, State University of New York, Albany.

Sikand, Y. (2010), 'Understanding Islamic Feminism: An interview with Ziba Mir-Hosseini', *MRZine*, 9 February, mrzine.monthlyreview.org/2010/sikand090210.html.

Singleton, A. (2014), *Religion, Culture and Society: A global approach*, Sage, London.

Spielhaus, R. (2012), 'Making Islam Relevant: Female authority and representation of Islam in Germany' in Masooda Bano and Hilary Kalmbach (eds), *Women, Leadership, and Mosques: Changes in contemporary Islamic authority*, Brill, The Netherlands.

Steuter, E. (1992), 'Women Against Feminism: An examination of feminist social movements and anti-feminist counter-movements', *The Canadian Review of Sociology and Anthropology*, vol. 29, no. 3, pp. 288–306.

Sultan, W. (2009), *A God Who Hates: The courageous woman who inflamed the Muslim world speaks out against the evils of Islam*, St Martin's Press, New York.

Swindle, D. (2010), 'Feminist Hawk Rising!' *NewsReal*, 27 February, www.newsrealblog.com/2010/02/27/feminist-hawk-rising/.

The United States Census Bureau, 2014 Population Estimates (2015), 'Monthly Population Estimates for the United States: April 1, 2010 to December 1, 2015', factfinder.census.gov/faces/tableservices/jsf/pages/productview.xhtml?src=bkmk.

Treacher, A. (2003), 'Reading the Other: Women, feminism, and Islam', *Studies in Gender and Sexuality*, vol. 4, no. 1, pp. 59–71.

Trotman Reid, P. (1984), 'Feminism Versus Minority Group Identity: Not for black women only', *Sex Roles*, vol. 10, nos. 3/4, pp. 247–55.

Twenge, J.M. & Zucker, A.N. (2006), 'What is a Feminist?', *Psychology of Women Quarterly*, vol. 23, no. 3, pp. 591–605.

Tyson, L. (2015), *Critical Theory Today: A user-friendly guide*, Routledge, New York.

Van Sommer, A. & Zwemer, S.M. (1907), *Our Moslem Sisters: A cry of need from lands of darkness interpreted by those who heard it*, Fleming H. Revell Company, Edinburgh.

Wadud, A. (1993) *Qur'an and Woman: Rereading the sacred text from a woman's perspective*, Oxford University Press, New York.

— (2006), *Inside the Gender Jihad: Women's reform in Islam*, Oneworld Press, Oxford.
Webb, G. (ed.) (2000), *Windows of Faith: Muslim women scholar-activists in North America*, Syracuse University Press, New York.
Werbner, P. (2005), 'Honor, Shame and the Politics of Sexual Embodiment Among South Asian Muslims in Britain and Beyond: An analysis of debates in the public sphere', *HAGAR—The International Social Science Review*, vol. 6, no. 1, pp. 25–47.
White, A.M. (2006), 'Racial and Gender Attitudes as Predictors of Feminist Activism Among Self-identified African-American Feminists', *Journal of Black Psychology*, vol. 32, no. 4, pp. 455–78.
Wolcott, H.F. (2003), *The Man in the Principal's Office: An ethnography* (updated edition), AltaMira Press, California.
Yegenoglu, M. (1998), *Colonial Fantasies: Towards a feminist reading of Orientalism*, Cambridge University Press, Cambridge.
Zahedi, A. (2007), 'Contested Meaning of the Veil and Political Ideologies of Iranian Regimes', *Journal of Middle East Women's Studies*, vol. 3, no. 3, pp. 75–98.
Zine, J (2004), 'Creating a Critical Faith-Centered Space for Antiracist Feminism: Reflections of a Muslim scholar–activist', *Journal of Feminist Studies in Religion*, vol. 20, no. 2, pp. 167–87.
— (2006), 'Unveiled Sentiments: Gendered Islamophobia and experiences of veiling among Muslim girls in a Canadian Islamic school', *Equity and Excellence in Education*, vol. 39, no. 3, pp. 239–52.
Zine, J., Dei, G., & Wane, N. (2003), 'Dealing with September 12: Integrative anti-racism and the challenge of anti-Islamophobia education', *Orbit*, vol. 33, no. 3, pp. 39–41.
Zuckerman, P. (2003), *Invitation to the Sociology of Religion*, Routledge, New York.

INDEX

Abduh, Muhammad 31
Adrienne (pseud.)
　biography 45
　on domestic violence 93
　motivation for fighting sexism 76
　refusal to be trapped by double bind 118
　on support from her partner 91
Afghanistan, invasion of 14–15
Africa, nego-feminism 92
African-American converts to Islam 98
aid projects 28
Aisha (wife of Prophet Muhammad) 17
Al-Nisa'iyyat (Nasif) 19
Albrecht, Lisa 137
Alexander, Jacqui 137
Ali, Kecia 131
AltMuslimah 48–9, 79, 83
Aly, Waleed 93–4
Amani Services 59, 84
American Society for Muslim Advancement (ASMA) 50
An-Na'im, Abdullahi 133
Arab Feminist Union 19
Arabiat, Abdul Latif 28
Astarabadi, Bibi Kahanum 20
Ataturk, Kemal 31, 32
Australia, Muslim population 38–9
Azizah magazine 58, 80–1, 86–8, 119

Bad Ass Muslimahs 57
Badran, Margot
　on dichotomy between Islam and modernity 30
　on Egyptian feminism 31
　on Islamic feminism 33–4, 39
　on middle space between feminism and Islamism 127
　on Muslim views of fighting sexism 40
　on Muslim women as feminists 126–7
　on patrimonial home of feminism 19
　on secular feminism in the Middle East 35
　on secular feminism versus religious feminism 130
Baktiar, Laleh
　biography 54–5
　criticism of her scholarship 95, 99
　dismissive suspicion from other Muslims 98
　on domestic violence 120
　translation of Qur'an from woman's perspective 54–5, 73
Barazangi, Nimat 77, 135
Barlas, Asma
　biography 48
　on community attitudes toward fighting sexism 103
　on importance of theology 21
　on non-Muslim concerns about sexism 104

on projection of misogyny onto scripture 124
on working within an Islamic framework 134
'Believing Women' (Barlas) 48
benevolent sexism 24–5, 103
Beyond the Veil blog 50–1, 53
Blair, Cherie 15
Bunting, Annie 22–4
Bush, Laura 14–15

Canada, Muslim population 38
censorship 40, 109
censure of women, for challenging status quo 85–6
Chesler, Phyllis 14
colonialism, association with feminism 27, 28, 29–32
criticism of Muslim women's fight against sexism
   by Muslim men 89–90
   'Muslim women behaving badly' 94–7
   questioning of religious legitimacy of their work 95–6
   for 'shaming the community' 93–4
   suspicion of converts to Islam 98
Cromer, 1st Earl (Evelyn Baring) 14, 30

de facto feminism 34
discrimination, balancing and re-negotiating competing forms of 107–9
domestic violence 54–5, 65, 91–2, 93, 120
double bind
   balancing honesty and disclosure 121
   experienced by Muslim women 107–14, 115–16

as multiplied control 117
privileging of non-Muslim audience's perspective 121–2
refusing to be bound by 117–18
sexism and misogyny in gangsta rap 114–15
use and prominence of phrase 113
double jeopardy 113, 117
double-bind of performativity 116
Dreher, Tanja 116

East–West antagonism 30
Ebony magazine 80
education of women 18, 19, 22–3
egalitarianism 64, 66
Egypt
   modernisation 30, 31
   religious and secular approaches to feminism 131
   women's liberation 29–30
Egyptian feminism, history of 19–20, 31
Egyptian Feminist Union 19
equality, Western liberal concept of 26
'equality versus difference' debate 25

faith
   activism as expression of 81
   as tool for personal and social liberation 34, 66–7, 81–2, 128, 132
faith-centred approach 127–8, 131–4
faith-positive feminism 34, 35–6
The Fatal Feminist website 56
Fatima (daughter of Prophet Muhammad) 31–2
Fazaeli, Roja 21, 32
female genital mutilation 1–2

feminism
- colonialism and imperialism 27, 28, 29–32
- evolution of 136
- faith-positive feminism 34, 35–6
- and modernity 30
- Muslim resistance to 4–5, 26–34, 63, 89
- non-Muslim women's resistance to 89
- second-wave feminism 137
- and secularism 27–8
- third-wave feminism 136–7, 143
- *see also* Islamic feminism; secular feminism

Feminist Hawks 14, 28
Finch, Janet 44
Fiske, Susan 24–5
folk devils 15
freedom of speech and press 40

gangsta rap 114–15
Ghayda (pseud.)
- on double bind 108
- biography 50–1, 53
- on non-Muslims' responses to Muslim women's activism 104
- on utility of Islamic framework 128

al Ghazali 78
Glick, Peter 24–5

Haddad, Yvonne 71, 73–4
Hakimah (pseud.)
- biography 51
- on the double bind 118
- personality and motivation 74–5

Hanoum, Zeyneb (pseud.) 13, 112–13
harems 12–13
Harris, Colette 96
Hassan, Mona 90

Her Honour (Quraishi-Landes) 47
Heywood, Leslie 137
Al-Hibri, Azizah 132
Hidayatullah, Aysha 113
hijab
- legitimacy associated with wearing of 95–6
- state prohibitions on 31, 32
- Western obsession with 8, 16

Ho, Christina 113
honour killings, in Jordan 23, 28
hooks, bell 114
hostile sexism 24
husbands, support for women's activism 91
Hussein, Shakira 113

Ibn Kathir 16–17
identities of Muslim women, defining 7
Inside the Gender Jihad (Wadud) 33, 46, 68–9
insider's perspective 7–8
Iran
- gender activists use of religious arguments 134
- Islamic Revolution 20, 31–2
- modernisation 32

Iranian feminism 20, 31–2, 134
Islam
- assumptions and generalisations about 7, 9
- support for feminist ideals 126

Islam–modernity dichotomy 30, 40
Islamic Action Front (Jordan) 28
Islamic authenticity 131
'The Islamic Bill of Rights for Women in the Bedroom' (Nomani) 47
'The Islamic Bill of Rights for Women in the Mosque' (Nomani) 47

Islamic feminism
  in Egypt 19–20
  emergence at national level 18–19
  in Iran 20
  methodology 135–6
  resistance to term 'feminism' 26–34, 127
Islamic knowledge, women's production of 71–2, 77, 79, 109
Islamic law, rights and status of women 12
Islamic Outreach Foundation 63
Islamic Society of North America (ISNA) 52
islamofascist misogyny 14
Islamophobia 15, 107, 109, 112, 114

Jessica (pseud.)
  biography 53
  criticism of her work 94–5
  on differential treatment of women 97
jihad, meaning of 145
Jordan, honour killings 23, 28
jummah, female-led 47

Kandiyoti, Deniz 25
K.A.R.A.M.A.H.: Muslim Women Lawyers for Human Rights 132
Karima (pseud.)
  biography 53–4
  experience of criticism 94
  lack of community support 102
  on treatment of women 97
  on wearing of hijab 95–6
Khan, Daisy 50, 120–1
Khan, Sara 108
al-Khayyat, Sana 96
King, Deborah 117
knowledge production 71–2, 77, 79, 109

Latifa (pseud.)
  biography 55
  on community attitudes toward fighting sexism 103
  lack of community support 100–1, 102
  on managing Muslim sensibilities and non-Muslim attitudes 111
Letherby, Gayle 7
liberation of Muslim women from Islam 13–16
Love, InshaAllah (Mattu) 49, 91

Mackillop, Mary (Saint) 101
The Magazine of the Young Woman 19
Mahmood, Saba 14
Malika (pseud.)
  biography 55–6
  on community attitudes toward fighting sexism 102, 103
  on domestic violence 91–2
marriage, valuing of 27–8
Mattson, Ingrid
  biography 52–3
  openness and authenticity 119–20
  support from her husband 91
Mattu, Ayesha
  biography 49–50
  condemnation of her book 95
  experience of criticism 94
  on reconciling Islam and feminism 136
  on support from her husband 90–1
  support from women 88
medieval period, Muslim women's role and status 18
methodology 6, 7–8
Misciagno, Patricia 34
modernity, feminism and 30

mosques
	exclusion of women 61–2
	inclusion of women 9, 51–2
motherhood, valuing of 27–8, 32
mothers, influence on daughters 75
motivations for fighting sexism
	desire to amplify women's voices 62, 65, 68, 69, 70, 73, 75, 80–1
	dissatisfaction with status quo 62, 64–5, 66, 69, 70–4, 76
	key motivators 62
	negative experience as to search for 'true Islam' 62, 66–7, 69, 75–9
	personal history of fighting injustice 62, 63–4, 69, 74–5
multiplied control 117
Musa, Mabawiya 19
Muslim community/communities
	attitudes toward fighting sexism 102–4
	conceptions of 27–8
	diversity 27, 40
	gaining membership of 97–8
	population growth in Australia and North America 38–9
	resistance to activism by women 65
	veneer of unity 93–4
Muslim Matters website 52
Muslim women
	as embodiment of 'the other' 13
	importance of reputation 96
	rights and status under Islamic law 12
	silencing of 117
	stereotypical representations 39–40
	as victims of racial abuse in Western countries 114
	Western representations of 12–16
	see also sexism against Muslim women

Muslims for Equality and Human Rights (MEHR) 45

Nadwi, Mohammad Akram 18
Nasif, Malak Hifni 19
nego-feminism 92–3
Nigeria, promotion of women's rights through *sharia* 22–3
Nisa, Nahida
	biography 56
	motivation for fighting sexism 76
	on need to reclaim religious texts 132–3
	on religion as key to liberating women 81–2, 132–3
Nnaemeka, Obioma 92
Nomani, Asra
	accused of shaming the community 93
	biography 47–8
	on community attitudes toward fighting sexism 103–4
	on the double bind 117–18
	secular feminist perspective 137–8
	support from women 88
Nouraie-Simone, Fereshteh 39

objectification of women 66
Okoye, Ify
	biography 51–2
	motivations for activism 83
	on non-Muslims' responses to Muslim women's activism 104
	'pray-ins' 61–2, 93
	protests against exclusion of women from mosques 61–2, 78, 83
	on resistance to feminism 89
	on support from women 88
Orientalism 113, 126–7

'the other', Muslim women as
    embodiment of 13
'Our Moslem Sisters' (conference
    proceedings) 30
Outlaw Culture (hooks) 114–15
outsider's perspective 8

paedophilia 118
participants in study
    Australian's request for anonymity
        43–4
    biographies 45–60
    characteristics 42–3
    deaths of 60
    differences between Australians and
        North Americans 99–100
    selection 42–3
'Patriarchal Bargain' 25
Pearl, Daniel 47
'pray-ins' 61–2, 93
public debate, Muslims' engagement
    with non-Muslims 116

Quraishi-Landes, Asifa
    on argument put to Muslim
        community 111
    biography 46–7
    on false dichotomy of pro-Islam
        versus pro-women 127
    on pro-faith and secular feminism
        frameworks 128–30
Qur'an
    egalitarian nature of text 124
    English translation from woman's
        perspective 54–5, 73
    interpretations 124
    reading as patriarchal text 124–5
    verses pertaining to justice or
        women's rights 17, 22, 35
Qur'an and Woman (Wadud) 46, 89

racism
    intersection with patriarchy
        113
    intersection with sexism
        113
Ramadan, Tariq 38
rape victims, treatment of 129–30
religiosity, and benevolent sexism 25
religious currency 131–2
reputation, importance for Muslim
    women 96
Reshad, Fatma 19
Roald, A.S. 21
Rose, Tricia 117
Rouse, Carolyn 97–8
The Runnymede Trust 15

El Saadway, Nawal 20
sacred texts, re-reading and
    re-interpreting of 35, 40, 46, 125,
    133–4
Sakina (great-granddaughter of Prophet
    Muhammad) 17–18
Sandoval, Chela 137
Sarah (pseud). 57
Schüssler Fiorenza, Elisabeth 76–7
second-wave feminism 137
secular feminism
    in the Middle East 35
    as only approach to tackling sexism
        126–7, 137–8
    utilising when appropriate 128–31
secularism, association with feminism
    27–8
Segrest, Mab 137
sexism
    benevolent sexism 24–5
    hostile sexism 24
    as inherent in Islam 125–6
    intersection with racism 113

sexism against Muslim women
    history of Muslim women's struggle against 16–26
    ignorance and arrogance regarding 1–4, 6
    Islam as cause of 5
    motivations for pushing back against 62, 69
    religiously framed approaches to challenging 21–2
    Western Muslim women's fight against 5–6, 9–10
    within Muslim communities 9
Sexual Ethics and Islam (Ali) 131
sexualisation of women 65–6
Shafik, Doria 19
Shaikh, Sa'diyya 7, 70–1
Sha'rawi, Huda 19
shariah
    meaning of 142
    using to fight dangerous patriarchal practices 22–3
Shia Muslims 98
shirk 76
Singleton, Andrew 123
Standing Alone in Mecca (Nomani) 47–8
Stockholm Syndrome 76
The Sublime Quran (Baktiar, trans.) 54
Sunni Muslims 98
support for Muslim women's activism
    in Australia 100–2
    differences between Australia and North America 99–100
    from Muslim men 88, 89–91
    from Muslim women 88–9
    from non-Muslims 88
    from younger women 88–9

Taherah Qurrat-ul'Ayn 20
Taj-ul Sultanah 20

Taylor, Tayyibah
    biography 58
    desire to amplify women's voices 83
    on the double bind 118–19
    investigation of faith 83
    on Muslim reactions to *Azizah* 86–8, 99
    pro-faith stance 128
    on women's self-definition and validation 80–1
teaching roles in Muslim community 68
Thatcher, Margaret 63
third way 127, 136, 143–5
third-wave feminism 136–7, 143
Treacher, Amal 133–4
Turkey, secularism and feminism 31

Uddin, Asma
    biography 48–9
    on the double bind 120
    motivations for fighting sexism 78–9, 83
Umaymah (pseud.)
    biography 58–9
    on community attitudes toward fighting sexism 102
    on relationship between feminism and Islam 128
    support from women 88
Umm Salamah (wife of Prophet Muhammad) 17
ummah 37–8
underage marriages 22
United States, Muslim population 38

Waajida (pseud.)
    biography 59
    on community attitudes toward fighting sexism 102, 103
    on confirming stereotypes 110

on constraints on what can be said 110
on dealings with non-Muslims 109–10
on importance of reputation 96
motivations for fighting sexism 62–8, 82, 83–4
pro-faith stance 128
spiritual imperative 82
on support from Muslim men 90
on women speaking for themselves 80
Wadud, Amina
accused of being anti-Islamic 33
biography 45–6
challenging of her membership of community 98
criticism of her activism 85–6
on gearing presentations for different audiences 109
imperative to challenge sexism 40–1
on pro-faith feminism 135–6
rejection of feminist tag 29
re-reading of sacred texts 72
on risking criticism 68–9
on support from younger women 88–9
Wahabi-salafism 109
'War Against Islam' 28
Webb, Gisela 41

Western Islamic discourse 39
Western views of Muslim women, historical overview 12–16
Western women, conversion to Islam 8, 42, 98
What if Shariah weren't the Enemy (Quraishi-Landes) 47
Woman and Sex (Saadway) 20
women's empowerment in Muslim communities, political overlay 28
Women's Islamic Initiative into Spirituality and Equality (WIISE) 50
women's liberation, in Egypt 29–30
women's rights in Islam 26
womanhood, Muslim women as inverse of Western ideal 13

Zafreen (pseud.) 60
motivation for fighting against sexism 74
on non-Muslims' responses to Muslim women's activism 104–5
pro-faith stance 128
support from younger women 88
on wearing of hijab 96
Zayd (husband of Sakina) 18
Zennour, Hadidje 13
Zine, Jasmin 7

OTHER GREAT TITLES FROM MUP • OUT NOW

Dear Quentin
Letters of a Govenor-General

Quentin Bryce

ISBN 9780522871166(hb)
ISBN 9780522871173 (ePub)

As Australia's first female Governor-General, Quentin Bryce handwrote more than fifty letters each week. She wrote to those she had met and connected with as her role took her from palaces to outback schools, from war zones to memorials, from intimate audiences to lavish ceremonies. She received even more letters from every corner of the country. Generous, witty and always heartfelt, her letter-writing skills were honed at boarding school, from where she would write to her parents every Sunday.

Dear Quentin is a rich collection of the letters the Governor-General wrote and received during her six-year term to prime ministers Rudd and Gillard, Mark Donaldson VC, pals Anne Summers and Wendy McCarthy, Indigenous elders, war vets, Girl Guides, grandchildren, as well as the proud owner of a calf called Quentin.

Royalties from this book will be donated to Murdoch Childrens Research Institute, making a real difference to child health through world-leading research and disease prevention.

MUP
BOOKS WITH SPINE
www.mup.com.au

OTHER GREAT TITLES FROM MUP • OUT NOW

Take Heart
A story for modern stepfamilies
Chloe Shorten

ISBN 9780522871326 (pb)
ISBN 9780522871333 (ePub)

These days, families come in all shapes and sizes. They move from one state to create a family in another. They combine into new homes, take holidays with blends of children and parents from different households. They invent routines and rituals to establish their own rhythms. And don't forget the double sets of school uniforms and pyjamas under different roofs.

Welcome to the new normal of family life for many Australians.

It is a path Chloe Shorten has walked. Chloe was surprised at the lack of helpful information and unexpected tripwires for those not fitting the traditional cookie-cutter model. She was also heartened by the sensible advice she unearthed, the resilience of her children and the joy of watching her husband become a father three times over.

Chloe tells of her own quest to create a new normal. Honest, sincere and warm-hearted, this is a story of the modern household and explores the idea of who qualifies as 'a family' in the twenty-first century.

MUP
BOOKS WITH SPINE
www.mup.com.au

OTHER GREAT TITLES FROM MUP • OUT NOW

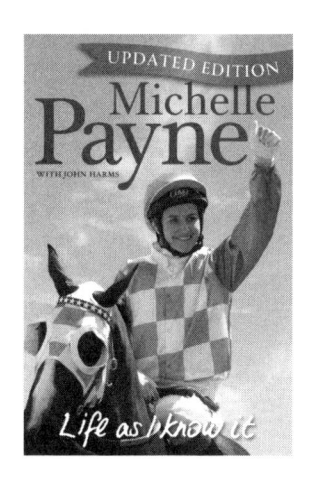

Life as I know it
Updated Edition
Michelle Payne

ISBN 9780522870169 (pb)
ISBN 9780522871609 (ePub)

In *Life As I Know It*, Michelle Payne tells her deeply moving story. It will lift your spirits, stir your heart and give you courage.

Michelle was six months old, the youngest of eleven children, when the amily was hit with the tragic death of their mother, Mary. Their father, Paddy, a renowned horseman, raised his children alone. As a family, they all took on the daily demands of racehorses and a dairy farm as well as school and work. Family meant everything.

Michelle was put on a horse aged four. At five years old her dream was to win the Melbourne Cup. At thirty she rode into history as the first female jockey to win the Cup on the outsider, Prince of Penzance. Her strapper was her brother, Stevie. So when she declared that anyone who said women couldn't compete with men in the racing industry could 'get stuffed', the nation stood up and cheered. It was a moment that inspired everyone who dreams of beating the odds.

Michelle's hallmark grit and determination were needed in the year after her historic win. She took out her jockey/trainer licence while continuing the punishing regime of being a jockey. But a dramatic fall resulting in a split pancreas meant her year was filled with more rehab and reflection than rides.

MUP
BOOKS WITH SPINE
www.mup.com.au

OTHER GREAT TITLES FROM MUP • OUT NOW

My Way
Moana Hope

ISBN 9780522871524 (pb)
ISBN 9780522871531 (ePub)

Moana Hope is one of fourteen children. No fan of dolls or dresses, footy has always been her passion, and she would spend hours playing kick-to-kick with her dad and brothers at the local park. When her father was diagnosed with terminal cancer, Moana cared for him until his death four years later.

Footy and cricket provided an escape from the demands of domestic life, and she made state and national teams for both sports. She also began to explore her Maori heritage, getting tattoos that represented the dearest people in her life.

But as women's football became more popular, being good at the game wasn't enough—players started being pressured about the way they looked. Moana refused to grow her hair or cover her tatts, and for the first time in her life felt sidelined by the game. But later, inspired by a women's exhibition game, she realised what she was missing and returned with gusto to the game she loved.

As a powerful full-forward who can thrill crowds by taking big marks and kicking spectacular goals, Moana was signed by Collingwood as one of its two marquee players for the inaugural AFL Women's competition in 2017.

A high-flying athlete who is grounded by remarkable selflessness, Moana Hope is an inspiration for women and girls everywhere.

My Way is her story.

MUP
BOOKS WITH SPINE
www.mup.com.au